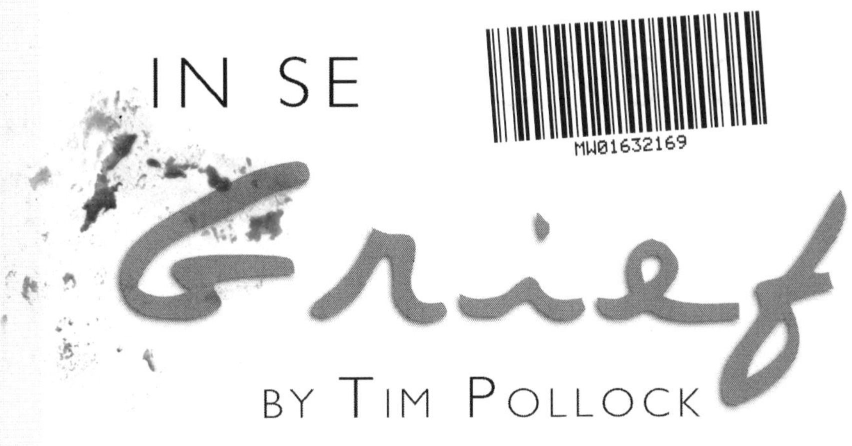

Wisdom's Way

Publications

www.wisdomsway.org

Publications
www.wisdomsway.org
Bible Literature Ministry of

The Home Church
11451 N. West Ln.
Lodi, CA 95242
(209) 339-7333
www.thehomechurch.net

Publication 2016

Dedication

To the blessed Holy Spirit and unrivaled Word of God for ministering grace upon grace upon grace to me during my darkest hours – You are always there.

Acknowledgement

A small host makes this book possible. Without my church family and immediate family I would NEVER have made it. My friends and colleagues – Rev. Eugene Haden, Rev. Mike Robinette, Rev. Paul Null, Rev. Jim Armor and Rev. Paul Tsika were invaluable with their prayer, insight and encouragement.

Beth Ridge is an amazing and dedicated transcriber and graphic designer. A special thanks also goes to Nancy Craig and Jason Turcott for their wise proofing and gracious comments, as they muddled through the maze. And finally much praise goes to my wife Pauline, who came along side and ministered to me in so many ways.

Contents:

Preface

By profession I am a public person, but by nature sharing things that are close to my heart is definitely not easy. And yet it is with the greatest joy that I share my soul.

Everyone grieves, you either will grieve in the future or you are presently grieving. Half of all married people will go through the gut wrenching pain of losing their husband or wife. I am convinced that there is a huge need for a fresh retelling of Job's story as seen through the eyes of lament. This book, In Seasons of Grief, is passionate but at the same time; compassionate. I've been there. I've wept day after day for months and yet can say I am in love with Jesus more than ever.

My suggestion to you if you are currently getting through the loss of a loved one, is to take a chapter a day and let the truth and grace of God's Word touch you. Read and reread the Scripture associated with each principle and let the heart of Job be yours.

Please know that I am praying for all that receive this book, may God speak peace into your heart.

Enjoy this powerful poem from a fellow lamenter.

Mourning Into Dancing

I should dance in God's presence, they say, though my heart is burdened with grief.

I should revel in God's mercy, they say, though my life is shattered with pain.

My partner has died.
This is the dark night of my soul.

Days and months press on.
Evenings and mornings lumber past.

My grief is great; my soul cries out,
"Why me, O God? Why me?"

"Not you, my child. Not you.
Your spouse has died. Not you

I gave you life. I gave you joy.
I can give again."

Sabbath.

Rest now, and begin again.

The sun burns brighter – so slightly brighter.

The pain of the grave becomes the power of grace.

Step by step, God works His miracle.

You shall dance again, my child.

You shall dance again.

You, O God alone, can turn

My mourning into dancing.

R. De Vries

Introduction

The topic of adversity is where the rubber meets the road for a Christian. Developing an unwavering trust in God's love and wisdom is where our theological theory becomes reality. You can only fake spirituality for so long in the face of intense pain! When your heavenly Father allows a season of failure, abandonment, betrayal, rejection, or deep loss...and when the pain is so great that life itself looses its meaning, then learning the life principles that Job acquired is the *only* way you are going to make it.

There are times when living God's way simply does not make sense. And in fact, even worse, it almost seems unfair. It takes patience...it takes trust...it takes HOPE in a loving God to get an eternal focus. When you can say like Job, *"Though he slay me, yet I will trust in him" (Job 13:15),* you will have found the secret of advancing through adversity!

Together, we are going to take a jet tour through the book of Job. Job, the oldest book in the Bible, is really about the love of God. During our journey we will learn to trust a loving God as never before. We will see beautiful jewels of truth that remind us to hope in God and Him alone. We will learn patience. We will see that no matter what is thrown at us, we *can* and *will* endure.

How long does it take for you to lose hope? For example: If you are standing in line, how long will it take before you get irritable? Human behavioral studies have found that the average time is 17 minutes. If you are on the phone, it is 9 minutes. Women lose their patience after waiting in line in about 18 minutes. For us men it takes less time before we get tense – only 15 minutes. People with a lower income and less education are more patient than those with a college education and higher income. People that live in suburbs and rural areas are more patient than those who live in an urban city. So, I guess then if you are a well-educated, wealthy man, living in the city...watch out! Truth be told, *everybody* looses their patience and gets wired.

Learning to handle troubles God's way then is the key.

The brother of our Lord Jesus, James, used Job as a premier example of enduring trials wisely. *"Ye have heard of the patience of Job, and have seen the end of the Lord; that the Lord is very pitiful, and of tender mercy" (James 5:11).* I wish I could say that I am always on top and winning in life, but honestly, at times I am simply "enduring." But actually, godly enduring *is* winning.

Sometimes in life, stuff is thrown at you that is so deep, so hard, so intense, that it may not be humanly possible to be on top. But what we *can* do is endure! We *can* have patience. We *can* have hope. We *can* trust the love of God. We *can* trust the wisdom of God. We can know that He is a great God! In the book of Job, we have seen the end of the Lord's mercies and that helps...that really helps. Asaph stated how helpful it was to go in the temple and see the *"end of the matter" (Psalm 73:17).* When you look at the "end result" of someone that endures adversity God's way, you will see a heavenly peace.

Job is the original "comeback kid." I'm glad that God is the God of restoration! Throughout scripture God paints Himself as one who rebuilds lives. People thought David was gone, but he wasn't! They thought Abraham was out of it, but he wasn't! Many thought Moses was done, but he wasn't! May God give us the understanding that no matter how bad it is, we can make it by God's grace!

As we come to the book of Job, we must understand that this is a man that went through incredible pain and a wide assortment of misery. It involved the personal loss of loved ones and health issues all the way to business reversal. But through it all Job blesses God. At times he loses sight of God's ways and gets grouchy, but overall we see him remaining patient and humble.

A little theological understanding is very important as we begin the book of Job. While the Bible is without error and infallible, not everything recorded in it is truth. For example, what Satan says is not true. Also what some of the people in the Bible say is not especially 100% true. But what they said is *reported 100%* truthfully. When you come to the book of Job, there are a lot of different ideas and concepts that are verbalized both by Job and his friends. You have to practice good Biblical interpretation in order to truly understand if those ideas represent God's mind.

This is not a book for the novice. It's a book that you can't just read through casually and get it. If you want to mine the depths of this rich ore, you must constantly adhere to sound Biblical interpretation. It is absolutely vital then, as you travel through the book of Job, that you compare its verses with verses in other books of the Bible. If you cannot find a supporting doctrine in another part of the Bible, then we must be very careful of holding our point of view too adamantly. No truth is of "private interpretation" as Peter said *(2 Peter 1:20).*

We must also practice context. The statements

uttered by Job's "friends" may contain truth or they may not, depending on context. If you keep that in mind when you are going through the book of Job it will be a wonderful, life-changing journey. It is a powerful book that reminds us of how incredibly sovereign God is and how that through enduring, we will come out with the blessing of God on our life.

Job is not a fictitious man. He is a real person. The book of Job is not some ancient fairytale that was just thrown into the Bible. The first three chapters of Job are pretty much a biography. These chapters could be best described by the first line in Charles Dickens book, *The Tale of Two Cities* – "It was the best of times, it was the worst of times." That sentence perfectly describes what we are about to go into as we approach chapter one.

Let's go to Job chapter one, where we are going to see the "big picture." *"There was a man in the land of Uz, whose name was Job; and that man was perfect and upright and one that feared God and eshewed evil" (Job 1:1).* Job *hated* evil. He was a man of solid character. In the midst of the all the junk that was constantly being thrown at him by the devil, and in light of all the accusations that people were saying and in the face of the silence of God, he maintained his integrity...wow! Where did Job get the power to keep on going? It was through his deep respect and reverence for God.

Job was blessed with a large and beautiful family, *"And there were born unto him seven sons and three daughters" (Job 1:2).* A large family is a wonderful privilege. Somehow God always takes care of them. God had been good to him materially as well, *"His substance also was seven thousand sheep, and three thousand camels, five hundred yoke of oxen, and five hundred she asses, and a very great household; so that this man was the greatest of all the men of the east" (Job 1:3).* His wealth didn't go to his head. He gave it all to God and was grateful for it. He knew it was just simply a blessing from the Lord. This was the "best of days", but the "worst of days" were coming.

Starting in chapter 1 verse 14, we are going to see in

rapid succession four dark messengers. *"And there came a messenger unto Job and said, The oxen were plowing, and the asses feeding beside them:"* Then in verse 15, *"And the Sabeans fell upon them, and took them away: yea, they have slain the servants with the edge of the sword; and I only am escaped alone to tell thee."* And further, see verse 16, "While he was yet speaking," (It's hard enough to have even one devastating loss), but then right on the heels of that one, he had another, *"there came also another and said, The fire of God is fallen from heaven, and hath burned up the sheep and the servants, and consumed them; and I only am escaped alone to tell thee."*

We see next that he had business loss, verse *17, "While he was yet speaking, there came also another, and said, The Chaldeans made out three bands, and fell upon the camels..."* Job has lost his transportation. He has lost his source of income. He has now lost precious friends. And then perhaps the darkest of all messages, Verse *18, "While he was yet speaking, there came also another and said, Thy sons and thy daughters were eating and drinking wine in their eldest brother's house:"* His children were having a family reunion of sorts, *"And behold there came a great wind from the wilderness, and smote the four corners of the house, and it fell upon the young men, and they are dead; and I only am escaped alone to tell thee" (1:19).* In just *one* day all was stripped away. One messenger after another had come. He now sits there with the rubble of his life lying all around him. He could see the *what,* but what he could not sense is the *why!* That's the real story of the book of Job. Why does God allow the righteous so much loss? God gives us a rare opportunity to look into the *why.*

In the midst of all the things that are going on – God Reigns! No matter what happens, Satan can only touch God's people by the permission of God. God is building character and trust into the life of each and every believer. God wants His children to be living examples of His Word. Strangely, it was in the path of obedience, and not disobedience that Job began to suffer his deepest trials!

Backing up a little we see in verses 6-12 of chapter 1 that Satan accused Job. That makes sense as he is the "accuser of the brethren" (Revelation 12:10). Satan is not in hell as some like to think. No…he is alive and well on planet earth (and heaven)! Ancient pictures show the devil down in hell trying to pull people in. Well, he is trying to pull people to hell but he is not *in* hell. He will be cast into the lake of fire someday, but he's not there now. In fact, the devil is in the greatest place in all the world – in heaven, among other places. That means that sometimes he's in youth meetings. Sometimes he's in Pastor's meetings. One thing you can be sure of is that he is actively attempting to dismantle your faith. What Job goes through in these 42 chapters of the Bible will give us 42 life principles on adversity.

Adversity Principle #1

It Is Not A Lack Of Faith To Express Human Grief

"Then Job arose, and rent his mantle, and shaved his head, and fell down upon the ground..." Job 1:20a

It is not wrong to express your grief and even to do so profoundly. In fact, it's healthy. One of the best things I did after my wife of thirty-four years, Lynette, died, was to weep deeply. It was not planned especially, but it happened often. Unknown to me at the time, I came to see that this was one of the most powerful and helpful things I could have done to move through the valley of death. Job rent his mantle. Do not bypass grief. Do not try to go around it, or go over it, and don't neglect it or forget it...enter into it deeply (friend, if you're going to cry, then really cry; if you're going to wail, then make good work of it).

"Lamenting" is a Bible doctrine. There's even a whole book in Scripture dedicated to lamenting (Lamentations). We have forgotten how to mourn in today's world. The modern church is all about happiness and joy, but lamenting should be part of the Christian life at times. How can we see the sin and misery that's going on in the world today and not lament? How can we not be brokenhearted over people dropping into a Christ-less eternity and not lament? How can we not lament over our own failures?

Honestly, I often wonder how it is that we could ever have joy. The great revivalist, Leonard Ravenhall said about Jesus, "If you saw Him you would've thought he was an older man." In fact, the common word on the streets during the ministry of Jesus was that He was fifty or sixty (*John 8:57*).

Grief has an emotional, mental, spiritual and even

physical effect on us. But it is normal and even necessary. Job was a great and godly man who praised God, but at the same time he "rent his mantle." He wept bitterly and deeply before God. Jesus also wept *(John 11:35).* Weeping is something so human and yet so divine. It is healthy when it's done right. It should never be done in self-pity, but because you are grieved in your spirit.

If you're going to cry, then really cry; if you're going to wail, then make good work of it

When a death takes place, you may experience a wide range of emotions, even when the death is expected. Lynette's four-year battle with breast cancer had many up's and downs. For the great majority of the time I felt as though we would just get through this trial, and she would be healed as she always had been before.

There was a point however, at about four or five months before her death, where God seemed to tell me that she was not going to get better. Even with that divine "heads up", I felt numbness at first, then denial, deep sadness, confusion and even despair after her death. I'm convinced that it is very important to allow yourself to express those feelings. For us emotional humans, death and deep financial loss are subjects that we like to avoid, ignore or even deny. At first it may seem helpful to separate yourself from the pain or ignore your feelings, but you cannot avoid grieving forever. Someday those buried feelings will need to be resolved God's way, or they may cause physical and emotional illness or even worse – spiritual weakness.

It's good to know that it is alright to pour out your heart to God. David wrote, *"I poured out my complaint before him; I shewed before him my trouble" (Psalm 142:2).* It is reassuring for me to remember that Jesus cares and is touched by my heartaches, *"For we have not an high priest which cannot be touched with the feeling of our infirmities..." (Heb. 4:15).* May I encourage you not to be embarrassed by your emotions then, just let it go. It is a necessary human emotion and not a lack of faith to lament.

Adversity Principle #2

Worship Is Always An Appropriate Response To Heartache

"Then Job arose...and worshipped," Job 1:20b

As Job was coming to terms with his loss, he wisely didn't leave God out of the picture. As hard as it was for him to sing, pray or praise, he availed himself of the healing power of worship. Some of the hardest, yet most inspiring moments of worship, for me occurred during the hardest of times. The raw emotions of sadness and loss can give you an eternal perspective. There is a sense of "coming to terms" with the reality that problems on this earth do end.

As Christians, we find assurance in the promises of

God's Word. Songs of worship that express these promises can be some of the most encouraging activities in a time of intense grief. Timely words sung at the right moment can bring a wave of comfort and release in God's faithful presence. Some of my most profound moments with God have been during these times, as tears would flow and faith would be expressed through prayer and song. Job spent time on his face worshipping God. There was no human to lean on...just he and God. True healing always takes place in the arms of God.

True healing takes place in the arms of God

Being in church after the death of someone you loved might be difficult at first. Certain hymns or songs, Scripture passages, or even just the physical presence of the sanctuary might bring overwhelming emotion to the surface. Most of the time, public worship is geared to joy, praise, and thanksgiving, which is far from your heart. But hang in there, as the joy *will* come back. The Holy Spirit will see to it that you can lament appropriately. Pray like David, that

God will restore your joy – "Restore unto me the joy of thy salvation…" (Psa. 51:12).

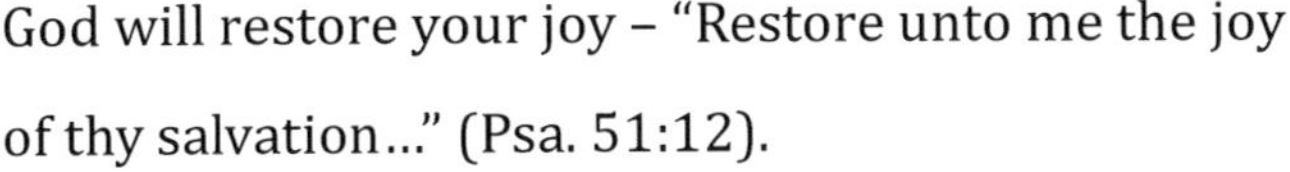

God is good even when times are bad!

When grieving people face tough issues, emotional worship is a cleansing release. Many a time I have put the headphones on, turned up my piano/cello instrumental worship and lost myself in deep sobs of wonderful expressions of praise. Yes…God is good even when times are bad!

Adversity Principle #3

Finding A Doctrinal Truth To Stand On Is Reassuring

"And said, Naked came I out of my mother's womb and naked shall I return thither: the Lord gave, and the Lord hath taken away; blessed be the name of the Lord," Job 1:21

Job got a word from God and held on to it! He testified to himself and others, "God gives, God takes away...it's His right to do what He wants." Job reminded himself that God owns everything. Humans own nothing. Everything is God's and He has the right to do with His stuff or people what He wants.

Loss involves grief, which is a natural response. As I have watched various Christians deal with losses over the years, it seems that too often we do not encourage grief, but instead we praise those who cover their feelings of sorrow. We seem to think that is a measure of their strong faith. We look at others and say, "He is so strong!" We are afraid to show our grief, thinking we lack trust. As a result, loss is a meaningless storm which causes many believers to blow away from God.

Paul told believers NOT to be tossed about by the storm, *"That we henceforth be no more children, tossed to and fro, and carried about with every wind of doctrine..." (Eph. 4:14)* If you don't stand on the doctrine of God you will surely fall into the depressing doctrine of devils!

Good doctrine anchors your soul to the rock when everything seems to be changing around you!

Don't explain away the hurt. Let the Book of books help you face the pain. Only the Bible gives seeds of hope for rebuilding your life. I simply would not have been able to make it without my Bible. In particular, I found great peace by praying the Psalms back to God. The Psalms are often filled with the raw emotional expressions of faith I was feeling. Verse by verse and out loud I would turn prose into petitions. Good doctrine anchors your soul to the rock when everything seems to be changing around you!

Adversity Principle #4

It Might Be A Sin To Wish For Death, But It Is Not Wrong To Wish For Heaven

"After this opened Job his mouth, and cursed his day.," Job 3:1

In Job chapters 2 and 3 we find insult being added to injury. Satan never quits. He is the sworn enemy of mankind and loves to attack even when a man is at his lowest. *"And Satan answered the LORD, and said, Skin for skin, yea, all that a man hath will he give for his life. But put forth thine hand now, and touch his bone and his flesh, and he will curse thee to thy face" (Job 2:4,5).* God allowed Satan to touch Job's body, but put a limit on it.

We read that some sort of skin disease progressed,

perhaps even cancer, so much so that his entire body became covered with open sores! He couldn't get any relief and had lost all of his money so he really couldn't hire any physicians. He also couldn't get any medicine. He had no servants that would come and help him. He couldn't sleep. What could a man do in such a terrible condition. He turned to the only thing that he could – he turned to his beloved mate. He hoped that his wife would reach out, and somehow comfort his body and spirit. But sadly she had gotten so upset and overcome because of all the loss and problems, she had a faith crisis of her own. She straight up told her husband to curse God and commit suicide *(Job 2:9)!*

And if that wasn't bad enough, now Job is going to have to endure the betrayal of friends. *"Now when Job's three friends heard of all this evil that was come upon him, they came every one from his own place; Eliphaz the Temanite, and Bildad the Shuhite, and Zophar the Naamathite: for they had made an appointment together to come to mourn with him and to comfort him. And when they lifted up their eyes afar off, and knew him not, they lifted up their voice, and wept; and they rent every one his mantle, and sprinkled dust upon their heads toward heaven. So they sat down with him upon the ground seven days and seven nights, and none spake a word unto him: for they saw that his grief was very great" (Job 2:11-13).* Now, to the credit of Job's friends they did at least come to visit Job in his sickness. I do not believe that they meant to betray...at least at first. I really think their motive was to come and somehow be a help to him. But as it turns out these friends got all caught up in the trash talk surrounding Job. They may have come with a good motive, but soon got infected from all the negative talk.

It may be a sin to be constantly wishing for death but it certainly can't be wrong to wish for heaven!

Finally, Job begins to speak up. In Job 3 we find Job's "death wish." He wishes he had not been born or at the least, that he had died at birth, *"After this opened Job his mouth, and cursed his day" (Job 3:1).* Most people have parties on their birthday but his grief was so profound that he "cursed" his birthday. This doesn't mean that he cursed God. It just means he wished that he had never been *born*. Now, you don't see Job wishing that he had ever been *born again*! He's thankful for his faith and his God. He was never bitter at God. He had seen all the good that God had done for him.

The words of Job are done in a poetical style. He is a cup that is brimming with pain and it can't help but spill over with copious words. He complained to God, "You could've saved everybody a whole lot of trouble if you had just killed me." Frankly, as you read through chapter 3, it appears as though he's obsessed with dying. It almost sounds like he wanted to commit suicide. But that's NOT what he is saying. It may be a sin to be constantly wishing for death but it certainly can't be wrong to wish for heaven! I really think that's where his heart was. He was longing for heaven! He basically was saying, "I want out of this place."

Paul mused in the New Testament, *"For I am in a strait betwixt two,* ***having a desire to depart****, and* *to be with Christ; which is far better" (Phil. 1:23).* Many people who are suffering from terminal illness, painful conditions, intense sadness or emotional pain have a "desire to depart." When Job "cursed his day" I think he, like Paul, was simply wanting to go to heaven who called that a "departure." It was as if he was in an airport waiting to leave on the next plane. It was not so much that he wanted to depart from earth, but that he wanted to be with Christ! Yes, he was tired of all the pain. He really wanted to be in the presence of Jesus and loved ones that have gone on. He desired to be done with sin once and for all.

Wanting to die and escape from suffering, whether emotional or physical, is a very human condition. Suffering is hard. When we are under the intense pressure of suffering, we sometimes feel like we simply can't go on any longer. But reassure yourself that heaven WILL come and a lot sooner than you think. Until then, you have a job to do!

Adversity Principle #5

Compassion Is What Our Fellow Believers Need

"But Job answered and said, Oh that my grief were throughly weighed, and my calamity laid in the balances together!" Job 6:1

In Job chapters 4-7 the betrayal begins. We find his friend, Eliphaz, showing up and stating his accusation, "Job, you must have sin in your life because suffering is a sign that people are sinning." He urged Job to go to God and find out what the sin was, so that he can get rid of the sin, *"Then Eliphaz the Temanite answered and said, If we assay to commune with thee, wilt thou be grieved? but who can withhold himself from speaking?" (Job 4:1,2).* I see a big problem with what Eliphaz assumes. Notice that he states, "*We've* all been talking about you and your situation." What his friends should have been doing was praying or helping, but certainly not gossiping.

He goes on in *Job 4:5*, *"But now it is come upon thee, and thou faintest; it toucheth thee, and thou art troubled."* Eliphaz says, "Now, I know you've had some problems lately that have been *touching* you." He uses the same phrase as Satan in chapter 1 who stated to God, "...let me *touch* Job." But it says something to me in that Eliphaz simply called Job's calamity, "trouble."

Job probably thought to himself, "Trouble? This is more than a little trouble...my life has been destroyed...everything I've held dear is gone. This is not a problem, it is a crushing blow to my entire life." Eliphaz appears to make light of the situation and then if that wasn't enough, in verse 7 he belts out a false doctrine. He is as sure of it as he can be, *"Remember, I pray thee, who ever perished, being innocent? or where were the righteous cut off?" (Job 4:7)*. Well, I can give you one innocent person that suffered, Christ! He speaks forth an "undeniable" theological truth, "good people never suffer." Now, that sounds good, but there's only one problem – it's totally false! His erroneous words were essentially the misguided doctrine of positive confession. There are people still today that say, "All you have to do is name it and claim it and it will be yours. If you are sick it's because there is sin in your life."

The real facts however are that it is God himself that allows sickness and death. God is a sovereign God and He does what He wants. I can't make God do anything. I can't demand that the Holy One stop the universe, reach down and do for me all the things I would like.

Empathy is the ability to enter into the heart and feelings of another person

Eliphaz thinks he has it all figured out. And then if that wasn't enough he claims to have received a vision, *"Now a thing was secretly brought to me, and mine ear received a little thereof" (Job 4:12).* Eliphaz states matter-of-factly, "I had a vision and I know that you've got sin in your life!" Oh, really? That's amazing that you've got it all figured out Eliphaz, you've got a doctrine, you've had a vision and you've been discussing Job's problem with people. It's sad when we see people that treat others with such a lack of mercy.

In Job chapter 5, Eliphaz goes for the jugular vein. He's going to get personal with Job. He's going to talk about his family. What kind of a friend will find a man when he's down and then talk about why he lost his children? In Job 5 he says, "Do you know why you lost your children? You are cursed because you have sin in your life!" Could you imagine a person saying that to someone who is grieving? *"I have seen the foolish taking root: but suddenly I cursed his habitation" (Job 5:3).* Here's a man covered head to foot with sores, he has lost his money, he has lost every friend he ever had and he has even lost his children. What Job needed was prayer not picking.

In Chapter 6 and 7 we see the summary of Job's response. It is simply this, "My suffering is what makes me want to die, *not* my sin." Job was not a bitter man, but he spoke very clearly to his friends, *"But Job answered and said, Oh that my grief were thoroughly weighed, and my calamity laid in the balances together!" (Job 6:1).* Job appeals to his friends to reconsider. He says in fact, "If you were really weighing the depth of my sorrows, you would not be thinking or talking like this." Now, it's true that Job speaks rather rashly, and I am not condoning that.

And I don't think that any Bible commentary supports all that Job says, but what he goes on to say in chapter 6 is profound: "It's easy for you to say these things as you're healthy. You're sitting there with a whole body and you're telling me that I need to trust God more? You have your nice family and your good job, your bank account is positive and your tummy is full. But I have nothing. I am just sitting here wishing I could die and go to heaven. I wish you would weigh my situation more thoroughly. Do you realize what it's really like to go through this?"

What Job is saying is that God's people need to have empathy. Empathy is the ability to enter into the heart and feelings of another person. The Bible tells us to "weep with those who weep" *(Rom. 12:15).* When a person's heart is broken, sending a cheerful card that says, "Smile, God loves you" is not likely to help.

We live in a funny culture today where people don't like to think about unpleasant things. The New York Times recently was called on the carpet for showing photographs of starving children in Africa on the front page. People complained that this was not appropriate for the front page. Why? It wasn't that they were naked or something like that. No, it was not appropriate to them because it made them address the reality of starving people. We don't like to deal with malnutrition when we're drinking our $5 Starbucks coffees...it bothers us. We don't like that. We don't like to deal with issues like that.

In chapter 7 Job will turn his voice to God and will speak openly and very vividly. In verses 11 and 12, he in essence asks, "God, who am I?" I can see Job on his face before God, crying out and saying, "God, who am I? Am I a monster? Why are you doing this? Am I some kind of an evil monster?" He just couldn't understand why he was in God's crosshairs. And then in verse 20 and 21 we see Job's great heart of humbleness, *"I have sinned; what shall I do unto thee, O thou preserver of men? why hast thou set me as a mark against thee, so that I am a burden to myself?" (Job 7:20).* My dear friend, *everybody* is having a tough day. Behind every smile is a broken heart. May God help us to humble ourselves, confess our faults and start reaching out to others like Job did.

It's often hard to know what to say or do when someone you care about is grieving. You may be afraid of intruding, saying the wrong thing, or making the person feel even worse. Or maybe you think there's little you can do to make things better. While you can't take away the pain of the loss, you can provide much-needed comfort of Christ's love and support. There are many ways – but often just small deeds of kindness are best.

The death of a loved one is one of life's most difficult experiences. Often, you feel isolated and alone in your grief. Don't let discomfort prevent you from reaching out to someone who is grieving. Now, more than ever, your prayer and support is needed. You might not know exactly what to say or what to do. You don't need to give a lot, if any, advice. The most important thing you can do for a grieving person is to simply be there. Not smothering them of course…just caring and praying.

Adversity Principle #6

God Is Still Wise, Loving And All Powerful No Matter How Much We Are Hurting

"He is wise in heart, and mighty in strength: who hath hardened himself against him, and hath prospered?" Job 9:4

When we get to the point in our personal journey where we can say that *we know* God is always wise and loving, then we know that we're graduating to university-level Christianity. There's one thing about emotional pain and that is this – you can't fake it for very long. But as the pain grows deeper and yet your faith grows stronger, you can know you are on the right track.

When our Heavenly Father allows failure,

abandonment, betrayal, rejection or deep loss and when the pain is so great that life itself loses its meaning. When, frankly, at times life doesn't seem fair and even perhaps God doesn't seem fair - it takes an unflinching faith in God's promises to carry on.

It takes an eternal focus to plow on during times of grief. It takes a sense that heaven is coming and there *will be* relief someday! The operational word through the entire book of Job is the word *faith.* Faith in God's love says that no matter what is thrown at us, we can and somehow will endure.

As we travel the pages of the book of Job we see him encountering many types of adversity, not the least of which are his so-called "friends." There is a story I heard about two redneck country boys. Billy Joe and his friend Bubba were out in the woods hunting when Billy Joe suddenly grabs his chest, keels over and falls to the ground.

Billy Joe doesn't seem to be breathing. His tongue is hanging out, and his eyes are rolled back in his head. Bubba frantically whips out his cell phone and calls

911 and yells to the operator, "Help! I think my friend is dead, what do I do?" The operator, in a calm and soothing voice says, "Calm down and take it easy. I can help. First of all, let's make sure that he's dead." There's silence and then a gunshot is heard. Bubba comes back on and says, "Ok, now what?" With friends like that who needs enemies?!!!

No human has ever had the assortment of miseries and terrible things happen in such a short amount of time as the man Job. And yet through it all, he just kept on believing. He had to move through the days of his life much of the time in darkness, but he kept trusting, putting one foot in front of the other. He kept blessing his God despite it all.

We're now going to move into the eye of the storm. After all that has happened in Job's life; in his family, finances and health - his "friends" heap coals of fire on him through insensitive remarks. They are going to try and convince him that the reason for his suffering is that there is sin in his life (certainly always a thought worth personal consideration, but these guys just won't let the thing go)!

Bildad, one of Job's friends, is hard-nosed, tough and reactionary. He heard Job's defense and will speak some correct things, however harsh. This is a great example of a person who has some good theology, but bad application. Benjamin Franklin once said, "Any fool can criticize, condemn and complain and most fools do." Foolish Bildad opens his mouth and lets it rip.

Studies have shown that the average person spends one-fifth of their life talking. If you were to take the words we say in a single day, it would fill a 50-page book. In a year's time the average person's words would fill 132 books, two hundred pages each! With many words, Bildad is going to assert, "You and your family are suffering because...well, I can't say it any other way, you're just a bad guy!" *"Doth God pervert judgment? Or doth the Almighty pervert justice?" (Job 8:3)* Of course it *is* true that God is just – it does not follow, however, that adversity is always God's justice being carried out. Tough times are not a guaranteed proof that a person has done something wrong. In Job, chapters 9 and 10, we will find Job's reply to Bildad and here's where we pick up some key life lessons on adversity.

No matter how much he was in pain, Job proclaims that he was still convinced that God was wise, loving and powerful. Job pleads, "Yes, I'm hurting and yes I'm having a tough time, but that doesn't mean God isn't wise and loving." *"He is wise in heart, and mighty in strength: who hath hardened himself against him, and hath prospered?" (Job 9:4)* No matter how much pain Job was in, no matter how overwhelming his circumstances were, whenever he had a chance to give God glory he stepped up, forgot his own situation and poured out his praise on his God! Job, in no uncertain terms, tells Bildad, "Do not interpret from my moanings about my difficult situation, that I am calling God bad, I'm just telling you I'm hurting."

Job concluded that since God is a God of power, wisdom and justice there is reason to trust that same God in times of suffering. Our loving Father

God knows the depths of grieving. God has suffered greater loss than anyone ever has. No one has lost more than our Father in heaven. No one has so continuously grieved over the pain of people gone bad; which is certainly worse than losing them to heaven (which is gain). No one has suffered like the One who paid for our sin in the crucified body of His own Son. It is this same God, who in drawing us to Himself, asks us to trust Him when we are suffering. You can trust Him precious friend!

Adversity Principle #7

As Finite Humans We Are Unable To Totally Understand God

"Which doeth great things past finding out; yea, and wonders without number" Job 9:10

It seemed as though Bildad and the others had God's ways all "figured out", but Job wasn't quite so sure. Job protests, "Look here, it's impossible to wrap your head around God." He told his friend Bildad, "Most of the time we don't have a clue what God is truly up to...and frankly, neither do you!"

"Life is not a problem to be solved, it is a mystery to be lived" - Adrian Ropers

Job was right, humans *can't* read the mind of God. There had been a private conference in the heavenlies between God and Satan back in chapter 1, that Job wasn't privy to. Had Job been given a head's up, he could have told Bildad with assurance that he did not know what he was talking about. Job's comments remind me of something the brother of Jesus wrote, *"But these speak evil of those things which they know not..." (Jude 1:10).* The fact is, things like the death of a loved one rarely make sense. We feel as though they died before their time or that they had so much left to do. Lynette died at the young age of fifty-two leaving me with five unmarried daughters. There was nothing about this that made any sense to me. She was greatly used by God and needed by all of us.

You also may have turned to God and asked why. And that just might be the time when heaven will be absolutely silent. But as Pastor Adrian Rogers said, "Life is not a problem to be solved, it is a mystery to be lived." That is what the book of Job teaches. We do not walk by sight but by faith. You just have to constantly...*constantly* be finding a promise from God's Word to live on. Job didn't know why all this happened but instead of walking away from God, he walked towards God in an attitude of trust. C. H. Spurgeon said, "God is too good to be unkind and He is too wise to be confused." A similar thought runs through a Christian chorus that says, "If I cannot trace His hand, I can always trust His heart." You can do this, friend!

When one who you love so dearly is taken away, then you know, just like Job discovered, that you *always* have God! God reduced Job down to nothing, and he learned that God was sufficient. You may never know why you had to suffer your loss. That's okay. What's important is that you know *Him*. You can and must trust Him!

Adversity Principle # 8

Nobody Can Claim Sinlessness

"If I justify myself, mine own mouth shall condemn me: if I say, I am perfect, it shall also prove me perverse." Job 9:20

It would be nice if there was a simple equation in life where we could consistently say a + b = c. But life is not that easily cut and dried. Yes, our sinful lifestyles can bring about trouble (think illicit drugs here). And I guess, if you want to be technical, there would be no trouble in the world if it were not for Adam and Eve's sin. Yet if the only time that I'm without any adversity in my life is when I'm totally sinless, that's never going to happen.

Job responded to his friend, "I know that the thing

you want me to do is to admit that I'm a sinner, repent and then all will be good." But he said, "I know the deceitfulness of my own heart." *"Though I were perfect, yet would I not know my soul: I would despise my life" (Job 9:21).* Job stated that when he really began to search his heart, he found baggage and junk there that he didn't know existed. He admitted honestly, "I'm going to get rid of every known sin, I'm going to repent and take responsibility for everything wrong but there are secret sins in me, things that *I* don't even understand, things so deceitful that I can't even recognize."

He doesn't require perfection on our part before God will work on our behalf

Job's point was simply this – if we say that we have no sin, we're just deceiving ourselves. "Bildad" Job reasoned, "You're deceiving yourself to say your life is without trouble because you have no sin. Everybody else knows that you have sin in your life, God knows that...and so do I!"

For me, the only thing I've ever found to do to

eliminate the possibility that my troubles are a source of divine discipline, is to is to throw myself at the feet of God in humility and say, "I am evil, sinful and I need your grace and your mercy and your help." I then try to make changes where I sense God's promptings. Only then I can face tough times with a clear conscience. We humans sin. In fact, we sin often; more often than we would like to admit. Because of this sad, but true, fact we need to clear the slate before we can be assured we will receive the help of God.

Jesus, in the "Lord's Prayer" reminded people to pray this very startling appeal: "Forgive us our debts..." According to this promise, we can ask God to carry away and cancel our spiritual debts. Is it really possible to expect God to pay my "bills", even when I've been foolish? The answer is yes! God may not do this in the way we expect, or in a way that eliminates all our pain. But He does promise to carry our load, even if we have blown it.

Typically, God does this by teaching us the principles

of His Word. He may on the other hand deliver us quite miraculously, even instantly. And quite often He uses both: wise long-term and miraculous short-term solutions. God cares, and he invites us to bring all our heartaches to him in prayer, and to present bold requests for him to meet those needs. God will take my *problems*, when I let him take *me*. Hallelujah, He doesn't require perfection on our part before God will work on our behalf.

Adversity Principle #9

It Is Easier To Know What To Do Than To Actually Do It

"If I say, I will forget my complaint, I will leave off my heaviness, and comfort myself: I am afraid of all my sorrows..." Job 9:27, 28

Job's friend, Bildad, had life all nailed down and clear, at least in his mind. He thought he knew all that needed to be done and how Job should handle his problems. But Job said that it wasn't so easy for him. He was confused and even afraid of sorrow. "The problem is," he told Bildad, "Sorrow and loss are tyrants and I can't do enough to get away from them." There was not enough food he could eat, there's not enough drugs he could take, there's not enough fun he could have...nothing took the pain away for more than a few minutes, at the most. When you are grieving, people will tell you that there's a bright side, but you know that there is not; you have lost everything. You don't know what you are going to do or how you are going to cope.

Even though I had five wonderful single daughters in my home, I found myself in need of companionship after Lynette's death. The overwhelming majority of people seemed understanding of that. But I received my share of icy reactions and sermonizing like, "You're married to Jesus now…you don't need a wife." I felt like saying, "That's easy for you to say. That's like a well fed man weighing 300 pounds, who's eating a big piece of chicken telling a man who weighs 98 pounds, that hasn't eaten for two weeks, not to be hungry!" It is a lot easier talking it than living it.

Bildad hadn't lost *his* wealth. He hadn't lost *his* family. He hadn't lost *his* health. Merciless people have it all figured out – exactly how people should respond and what others should do. But I'm telling you, sorrow can get beyond any of our platitudes. The feeling of loss can get beyond anything you've ever thought or dreamed of, it gets down into your very core. It is a whole lot easier to talk than to walk. It's kind of like the guy in Arkansas who got pulled over by the highway patrol officer and was quizzed, "You got any ID?" He replied, "'Bout what?" Oh my! Bildad had no ID! And frankly, many people today don't have a clue either.

We need God's wisdom and grace every day...you need it in your marriage, finances, work, ministry, children, parents, health, future and more. A young preacher wanted to preach in a robe. So the tailor took the measurements. He asked, "I need to know how long you've been in the ministry." "What does that have to do with it?" the young pastor questioned. "Everything – I've made a lot of robes, and if you're young in the ministry, you think you know it all. You walk around with your head held high and your chest stuck out...so I need to make it longer in front and shorter in back. But if you've been serving God a long time, you realize you don't know anything, you spend most of your time with your head bowed in prayer asking for wisdom, or on your knees looking to the only One who can help! You need it shorter in front and longer in back!"

Seriously, whatever you're facing, don't try to face it alone. Let's learn from Job – have mercy on yourself and others. And when you need wisdom, be quick to ask God for it.

Adversity Principle #10

Prayer Is The Best Medicine

"My soul is weary of my life; I will leave my complaint upon myself; I will speak in the bitterness of my soul. I will say unto God, Do not condemn me; shew me wherefore thou contendest with me." Job 10:1, 2

Job wasn't always correct in what he said or even how he said it, but he found genuine help in pouring out his heart through transparent prayer. You too will find relief in open and honest prayer to God – I certainly have. He learned that in the midst of everything that was going on to just keep crying out to God. Prayer *always* works.

The best thing that you can offer to any human is to pray for them

Sometimes people mistakenly think that having

patience is just sitting around calmly waiting for something to change. Nothing could be further from the truth! That is not patience at all. Patience is not passive. Patience is very active. It is just active in the *right* way! It is waiting on God in prayer and not moving until you get the go ahead from Him. Prayer *always* works.

I have got to believe that Job looked at Bildad and thought, "I am sure you want to help, but you know what, your lack of compassion and your words are *not* helping. If you really want to help me – pray. The *best* thing you can do for me is to pray. I need prayer more than I need your words." Because Job had had such a serious blow to his finances and emotions he had a lot of needs, but as much as he needed meals or phone calls he needed prayer more. Prayer – that's the kind of help that he really needed! Pray that God will speak, send peace and somehow turn things around for you.

Dear reader, I submit to each of you, the best thing that you can offer to any human is to pray for them.

A valuable thing that even a poor man can give is prayer. The healthy thing that a person who lies on his sick bed can give is prayer. The strengthening thing that a person who is older can give, is prayer and the one thing that we can all offer somebody is prayer.

I may not be able to give them my daytime, but I can get up early and pray for them. I may not be able to call them at Five o'clock in the morning but I can call to God. I may not have the resources to be able to go where they are, but I can always ask the Holy Spirit to go where they are. Prayer is the greatest thing we can do for our friends! Job pleaded with Bildad, "I know you want to get me right with God, and I am trying to do just that - but what I really need is prayer."

Losing a spouse is devastating – plain and simple. The lack of control and utter helplessness, the finality of death, the feelings of hopelessness, the minutes that feel like days are things only the Lord truly understands. And He does! Read the petitions listed in the book of Psalms. These are not the tidy little bedtime prayers of childhood. They are full of passion. I found (and still do) great…no, amazing comfort in praying the Psalms back to God. It is the *only* consistent relief I have found. People will sit next to you and talk of the weather or whatever – and it feels like they are far away. All I wanted to talk about was my wife. Every thought I had included her. Most of the time remembering her was comforting. But sometimes I felt like I couldn't stand thinking of her any more. There is *nothing* like losing a loving spouse, but I tell you that you *will* come through the valley. The world may never look the same but things will get back to a *new normal* (a good phrase to learn). Keep praying the Psalms!

Adversity Principle #11

Friends May Prove Unhelpful, But God Never Fails

"I am as one mocked of his neighbour, who calleth upon God, and he answereth him: the just upright man is laughed to scorn." Job 12:4

We are going to be introduced to some more of Job's friends in this chapter. If you thought Bildad's words were cruel, you're not going to believe his next friend, Zophar. Job's next friend, Zophar is just plain mean! Zophar, is thought to be younger. He certainly is brash (often a youthful misdeed). What he lacks in verbiage he will make up for in tone. There was not even one word of compassion given to Job. He just comes out blasting with his six-gun!

Job's friends had been sitting around for seven days and were tired of hearing him complain, moan and talk of wanting to die. They began to talk amongst each other. One person was saying one thing and then another. Pretty soon everybody was yakking. Today we call that gossip.

There was a three-year sociological research project at Indiana University that was conducted on gossip. The results were interesting, and surprisingly Biblical! They identified key dynamics about gossip. They discovered that it was not the *initial* statement that started gossip. Strangely enough, they said that the turning point in gossip was the *response*. For example, if the first person says, "So and so is a real snob" and if nobody seconds the motion, it dies. But gossip goes on because there's always a *second* person. Job's friends were chewing on him behind his back. Things went from bad to worse. Soon, they had tried, judged and convicted him!

It's always remarkable to me how someone can get mad at another without ever even talking and trying to substantiate matters. Not one time, do some of Job's "friends" try to reasonably clarify the issue. I've seen people leave friends of a lifetime without ever actually talking to them and getting the facts.

Zophar speaks pointedly, but ignorantly, *"Then answered Zophar the Naamathite, and said, Should not the multitude of words be answered? and should a man full of talk be justified? Should thy lies make men hold their peace? and when thou mockest, shall no man make thee ashamed?" (Job 11:1-3)* He doesn't say, "Job, I'm sorry about your situation." He doesn't say, "I'm praying for you." What does he say? He told Job that he talked too much and that must mean that he was guilty.

When you read the rest of chapter 11 you'll see more of the pious and ignorant things he says. His words were like the very plain Texan who stated, "A lot of preaching is longhorn preaching; a couple of good points with a lot of bull in between!" Ouch.

We find Job's wise response to Zophar, *"I am as one*

mocked of his neighbour, who calleth upon God, and he answereth him: the just upright man is laughed to scorn" (Job 12:4) Basically Job says, "You know what's really been so hard for me Zophar? One of the most bitter things for me is that the words that I'm hearing haven't come from an enemy, but it's coming from you guys…ones who I thought really cared about me." Job couldn't wrap his head around the betrayal. His heart was broken and the wound was getting deeper. What I've found over the years is that even though people will pull back on you, God never will. Sometimes unthinking people say hurtful things… let's make sure that we are not one of them.

What I've found over the years is that even though people will pull back on you, God never will

Sue Bohlin said on Bible.org, "It may be insensitivity or a lack of education that spurs people to say things to grievers that are unhelpful at the least or downright hurtful."

Sue says, "Don't start any sentence with "At least…"

- "At least he's in heaven now."

• "At least you have two other children."

• "At least you've had a good life so far, before the cancer diagnosis."

Don't attempt to minimize the other person's pain.

• "Cancer isn't really a problem."

Don't try to explain what God is doing behind the scenes.

• "I guess God knew you weren't ready to be parents yet."

• "This baby must have just not been meant to be."

• "Cancer is a gift from God because you are so strong."

Don't blame the other person:

• "If you had more faith, your daughter would be healed."

• "You are not praying hard enough."

Don't compare what the other person is going through to ANYTHING else or anyone else's problem:

• "It's not as bad as that time I…"

• "My sister-in-law had a double mastectomy and you

only lost one breast."

Don't use clichés and platitudes:

• "Look on the bright side."

• "She's an angel now." (NO! People and angels are two different created kinds! People do not get turned into angels when they die.)

What TO say:

• "I love you."

• "I am so sorry." You don't have to explain anything.

What TO do:

• A wordless hug.

• A card that says simply, "I grieve with you."

• Instead of bringing cakes, drop off (or better) send gift certificates for restaurants or pizza places."

I say amen to all of that! And pray. Then pray some more. It's the most powerful thing we can say or do.

Adversity Principle #12

Nobody Can Argue With God

"Behold, he breaketh down, and it cannot be built again: he shutteth up a man, and there can be no opening." Job 12:14

Job countered his friend's shallow theology with a powerful fact he was learning – God doesn't have to get our permission to allow adversity in our lives! He said it's a fool's pursuit to try to tell God what He can and cannot do.

Job tells Zophar in essence, "If I could, I would insist that God would stop. But I cannot tell God what to do. I've asked Him to stop but He just does what He wants. If I could avoid the pain I would, trust me. I would never knowingly do anything to bring this upon my family. If I knew what I was doing wrong, I would've changed it a long time ago. This pain that I'm having is simply unavoidable. It's in the path of duty. It's in my path of obedience."

Pain, for godly people, is sometimes unavoidable. Caution teaches us not do things that cause pain, and that's wise. But, when pain comes in the path of obedience you just have to plow on. Sometimes, part of the Father's plan includes loss and difficulty.

You do not need to see everything as good, but you do need to see things as working for a good purpose

If we try to avoid everything that's painful or hard we can't answer God's calling. If you say, "I can't get up early because I need my sleep, I can't go out and knock on a door for Jesus because I need my dignity, I can't have a large family because I can't afford that many children", then we misunderstand excellence. Anything good takes effort. Pain experienced in the path of duty is something that shifts our focus to God's power and gets it off ourselves.

It is easy to get irrational during times of grief. That is certainly understandable. But if we want to change how we feel and what we do, we need to change our *thinking*. Because many people have grown up believing that they are at the mercy of events and emotions, it's little wonder they develop negative thoughts. Grieving people need to challenge negative thoughts with the Word of God and make a realistic assessment of the situation. You do not need to see everything as good, but you do need to see things as *working* for a good purpose (Romans 8:28).

Pain experienced in the path of duty is something that shifts our focus to God's power and gets it off ourselves

In my life I have noticed that saying scriptural affirmations helps me maintain mental and emotional balance. Speaking the word of God fosters faith. Faith comes by hearing the Word *(Romans 10:14).* Yes, I am really saying to speak (or play it from one of those Bible apps) the Bible out loud. You will be amazed at the difference it makes. Do it today!

Adversity Principle #13

Life Has Ebbs And Flows

"He increaseth the nations, and destroyeth them: he enlargeth the nations, and straiteneth them again" Job 12:23

God does what He wants; He increases nations and destroys them. He also works uncontested in personal lives. Job reminds Zophar, "You really don't know what you're talking about. You're telling me that if I do this or that I'm going to make God stop inflicting this pain on me? Are you kidding? No, you don't get it Zophar. Every life has ebbs and flows. It's up one day and down the next. Last time I checked life wasn't a party!" Yes, I'm convinced the sooner we realize that life is not a party, the better off we will be, because then we learn to get the grace of God in order to make it.

For whatever reason, God in His sovereign and providential will knows when to make something flow freely and He knows when to pull back. God just does life how He wants. I've often thought to myself (and I'm sure you have too), "This problem is the last thing I need right now." Have you ever thought or voiced something like, "The last thing I need right now is a flat tire." But God doesn't listen to me! He simply does what He wants, when He wants. It is a fact – life has its ebbs and flows.

It's also uncanny to me how often our adversities come in a series, like Job's did. It seems to me if God could at least stretch them out, I could have some time to regroup. Then I could gather some strength and could take it better. But God doesn't care about *my* pacing! He cares deeply about my character though!

He wants so much to use me and make my life a public billboard of His grace, mercy, joy and peace.

He says to me, "Look Tim, I know you don't want pain, but trust me, you only have a few years to live and I have to make somebody a billboard of grace. You just happened to be on my list. You're going to be that person that I'm going to hammer. I'm going to file on you. I'm going to saw on you and I'm going to break you. But I tell you something wonderful – I am making a masterpiece and I will be there with you the whole way!"

Because we are human, our lives are going to be hammered by adversities like loss. Trust me, that's just the way life is. We can't stop the ebbs and we can't create the flows. We can't make things go up and we can't prevent things from going down. That's outside of our ability. We can get all the insurance we want, we can purpose that we will never get sick, we can say that we're going to be healthy all our life but my friend, cancer can happen to anybody. People who are strong and capable die in their 50's. People who are billionaires cannot stop heart disease despite their resources. Nobody gets a chance to make God do things, or make God *not* do certain things; life has ebbs and flows.

Grief happens to everyone at some point in life. Not only after the death of a loved one, but also after any major change such as losing a job, kids getting married, or moving. No matter the cause, grief is one of the hardest experiences of your life. It is emotionally, mentally, physically and even spiritually exhausting.

You will have some easier days and some very hard days. Don't be surprised if you are feeling better one day and wake up the next day feeling worse. Holidays, birthdays, anniversaries, music, even a scent can bring on the intensity of grief. This is normal. Be mentally prepared for the ups and downs by being forewarned. To be forewarned is to be forearmed.

Unfortunately, tough times are not merely an emotional experience. Bills have to be paid, belongings sorted, rooms cleaned out. All of these things can be overwhelming when you feel emotionally spent. Take life in bite size chunks. Make tasks line up one at a time. While grieving, you might not feel hungry, but be sure to keep eating fresh, healthy food so you will have the energy needed. Stress takes a physical toll. If you are healthy enough to do so, exercise regularly. Even just a short but regular walk will help. Jesus, during His earthly ministry, traveled mostly on foot. Maybe this was done mostly of necessity, but I wonder if it gave Him plenty of opportunities to take in plenty of fresh air, beautiful sights and sounds along with unhurried talks with friends and his Father in heaven. Just know that life has its ups and downs. By God's grace celebrate the ups and stay steady in the downs.

Adversity Principle #14

Have Some Mercy...You Might Be In The Same Situation Someday

"Is it good that he should search you out? or as one man mocketh another, do ye so mock him?" Job 13:9

Job brings perspective to the subject of adversity so well, "Zophar, let me ask you a question. What would happen if God searched *you* out? You've set a big standard for me. But could you hold to that same standard? If you were to go through what I'm going through, how would *you* react?" I say to all reading these words, myself included, I believe in justice, but we better have some mercy for people because each one of us, without fail, will be in the same place someday. Every one of us will go through a loss so deeply that it will be beyond our ability as a human to shoulder. That's the way life is. I cannot stop my troubles. I wish I could.

Job reminds Zophar that the standard he was holding him to, was also for Zophar personally as well. Job makes a very good point. We must be careful to make sure that we have mercy on others that are going through tough times. Life and loss are not as cut and dried as you might think.

I have accepted the high standards of the Bible for my life. While that is a good (great) thing, I know that at the same time, you can only do what you can do. We are all human, and God understands our limitations. Jesus while on earth got hungry, tired, sad, angry and was very human – but not sinful. Many of our issues are related to sin, but many are just because we are human. David had a good grasp of this truth. Speaking of Israel's shortcomings God stated, *"For he remembered that they were but flesh..." (Psa. 78:39).*

Not only do we need to give others a break, we need to go easy on ourselves. For example: before and after the funeral people are going to want to check in, call, drop by, and stop you on the street. Acknowledge that these things may be draining for you. Also, don't be surprised if their attempts at comfort, even from the Bible, don't especially help.

It's almost impossible to get a sanctified view of loss in the beginning stages of grief. Expect that you may feel more distracted or less productive than before your loss. Be understanding with coworkers, friends and even family. Take comfort in the fact that they mean well and are good-willed despite their shortcomings. You may find them feeling awkward around you. Let them know the best thing they can do is to just love you, be normal and pray for you.

You are forever different...but hopefully growing and accepting – even embracing – the fact that you will never be the same and that there is no end point to grieving

Realize that it will never be okay that your loved one died. Death is caused because of Adam and Eve's sin (and ours). It will be a great day when God eradicates death once and for all! *"And God shall wipe away all tears from their eyes; and there shall be no more death..." (Rev. 21:4)* Accepting this truth is one of the most freeing things you can do. Realizing that that you'll not get over this but carry it with you for the rest of your life is liberating. There is no magical answer to loss. It stinks. But someday...Hallelujah!... death *will be* abolished. Allow yourself to simply sit still with that reality.

I have heard people talk about having "closure." Honestly...I've never discovered how to do that. God says "love never fails" (1 Cor. 13), so how can the unfailing emotion you had for someone cease. No, I really think the grief stays – it just changes form. There's no end point to when you will be back to normal. You are forever different...but hopefully growing and accepting – *even embracing* – the fact that you will never be the same and that there is no end point to grieving. This will take a whole lot of pressure off of you.

You shouldn't feel pressured to dive head-first into life (or not to dive in) and to get back on track. Move ahead and pull back as you need to. Move as slow or as fast as works for you.

I know some people wondered how I could pursue a relationship after Lynette's death. All I can say is everybody is different. There is no "holy" time frame about when you should re-enter life and relationships. I read nothing in the Bible that tells how long one should wait to date after the death of your mate. All I know is that I longed for the sweet companionship again that had characterized our marriage.

There must be NO expectations put on people (or yourself) for that matter. Go easy on yourself. Do remember you are going through a physically and emotionally stressful time though. If you want the holidays to be the same as they always were, you are in for disappointment and frustration. No matter what you do, you will not feel as you once did. It will take time for you to adjust – maybe years, even decades, but I can guarantee that you WILL laugh again! God is a restorer, *"And I will restore to you the years that the locust hath eaten..." (Joel 2:25).*

Adversity Principle #15

Always Trust God Explicitly

"Though he slay me, yet will I trust in him: but I will maintain mine own ways before him." Job 13:15

Job reminded his friend that the only thing he could really do in life was trust God, *"Though he slay me, yet will I trust in him..." (Job 13:15).* Job had come to the point where he knew that if God was putting the knife to him, then the plan was to cut out some cancer, because God was a caring physician not a harmful attacker. He knew that if God should choose to permit a death in his life, it is His right. God is wise, just and loving and is only allowing this because it's going to be best. Now that's what I call trust.

When you get to the point that you are willing to

obey God, follow Him and love Him...regardless of the outcome, then no internal or external demon can beat that person! I love what the late English Pastor Charles Spurgeon says about this verse. He called it "God's slaying times." When it's "slaying times", then God is at work. When God's killing your finances, when He's killing the thing that you love so much, when He's killing your health...when it's slaying time, then He's got a plan for positive change! And if He has a good agenda then I will trust Him, however challenging.

We're never more like Christ than when we can go to our cross and can say, "though He slay me, yet will I trust Him." Jesus never sinned one time. He certainly didn't deserve the cross, yet His own father turned His back on Him. And yet He lifted up His eyes unto heaven and He said, "Father, I commend my life to you, Father kill me if that's what you need to do."

That's also what Isaac did to his own father Abraham. Job said in effect, "If God kills me then that's fine, I will not disobey Him, I will not call Him bad, I will not in any way think that He hates me, or I will not call Him unfair. God has the right to do with me whatever He wants; I'm just going to trust Him." That kind of a person makes demons run!

Job was telling Zophar, "If God kills me, that's fine but my young brother...do you understand what God is doing? Are you sure you've got it all down pat? I haven't stopped trusting God. I haven't quit being obedient to God. Yes, I am a dirt bag. Yes, I am a filthy sinner. In fact, I'm even worse than you think I am. But in no way, shape or form do I intend to disobey my God and I in no way want to call Him a bad God. He's a loving God. He's a great God and I'm going to trust Him regardless!"

May I say to each of you who are reading this... when your heart feels like it is going to shatter and hot tears are coursing down your cheeks, God does give us something worth trusting in during tough times – and that's Himself! Job reminded us, "I will trust HIM." The Lord has a plan to carry you through. When you are feeling so weak you cannot take another step, trust Him to hold you up, *"When I said, My foot slippeth; thy mercy, O Lord, held me up" (Psa. 94:18).*

This does not mean your heartaches will disappear, but it does mean you will have someone (God) beside you the entire way! Biblical trust is an absolute confidence in something you can't see, but know that somehow will work out. My friend, only Jesus can help. One day Jesus is coming back, and then He will set all of the wrong right. Know that nothing can or does happen without His loving approval. Rest in this knowledge! Trust Jesus!

Adversity Principle #16

Life Is Short And Difficult…But It WILL Change

"Man that is born of a woman is of few days, and full of trouble. He cometh forth like a flower, and is cut down: he fleeth also as a shadow, and continueth not. If a man die, shall he live again? all the days of my appointed time will I wait, till my change come. Thou shalt call, and I will answer thee…" Job 14:1-2, 14- 15

The title of this chapter may not be real sugary, but honestly, sometimes the only thing we can say during the tough times is, "Thank God, there is a better day coming!" *"Man that is born of a woman is of few days, and full of trouble" (Job 14:1).* There you go. There is every human's biography – life is short and life is tough, get used to it! Wow!

In fact, life is so short, it's just one series of issues after another, *"He cometh forth like a flower, and is cut down: he fleeth also as a shadow, and continueth not" (Job 14:2).* However, the Christian has this wonderful reassurance - there is a day coming when you are going to be changed. Life will change! 1 Corinthians 15:51 states that we shall all be *changed*. 1 John 3:2 states when you finally see Him (Christ), you will be *changed* to be like Him. Praise God! Brother and sister, this present life does not go forever. I'm not going to be here much longer. I'm leaving soon. One of these days I'm out of here. I'm going to be changed!

There is another change besides death. The Christian will be changed to have a resurrection body, *"Thou shalt call, and I will answer thee..." (Job 14:15).* Someday God Almighty is going to personally call your name, you will answer and rise out of the grave in the very flesh that you have now (though modified, thank God) – and you will see God. As a Bible-believing literalist, I believe in a bodily resurrection. I believe that just as Jesus was raised from the dead, and just as people could actually touch His hands and feel the scars and the hole in His side, so we will be changed and will be resurrected and will be given a new body, hallelujah!

Paul said, *"For now we see through a glass, darkly; but then face to face: now I know in part; but then shall I know even as also I am known" (1 Cor. 13:12).* Yes... known even as we were known. We'll get a new resurrected body but we will have a likeness to the same old body. It's really true! We will actually see our loved ones again!

My heart is often heavy. One of my friends has cancer and doesn't have a hopeful prognosis. Another friend's son was killed in an auto accident. I feel their deep grief. This world is ravaged by sin and death. It hurts. I know I'm not alone; anyone reading this has been affected by tragedy and heartache in some way. But know this...a better day is coming! I look forward to that day. I long for it. I hope you, too, find comfort from this promise of God.

I close this chapter with a wonderful story that you have perhaps heard before. The well-known hymn,

"It Is Well With My Soul", was written in the 19th century by Horatio Spafford. He lived in Chicago where he had a thriving practice as an attorney. He was intelligent and successful and had significant resources given to him graciously by God. He was also a friend of world-wide Evangelist D. L. Moody. But in 1871 he would begin to experience the fires of testing in his personal life that even to this day, more than 100 years later, we're still talking about.

A good portion of his money was lost in real-estate investments in the great Chicago fire. Several months before that, his only son had died. After having lost his money and his son, he, his wife and four daughters, planned a trip to Europe coinciding with one of Moody's meetings. At the last minute, Mr. Spafford could not go with his family and he sent his daughters and wife to go on ahead. Tragically, the ship that they were on was struck by an English vessel and within 20 minutes sank drowning all four daughters.

When his wife and a few survivors got to England, a

message was sent back, "Saved Alone." Mr. Spafford got on the next ship that he could and he began to sail across the Atlantic to get to his wife. The ship's captain, who had heard of his terrible plight, when he came to the very place that his daughters had drown stopped. There, Mr. Spafford wrote the familiar words, "when sorrows like sea billows overflow my soul, God has regarded my helpless estate, it is well with my soul." He didn't say it was well with his life, but he said it is well with my soul!

Sometimes in this life that is all we can really say, "it is well with my soul, everything is all right between me and Jesus." Life's not always so good but God is! A better day is coming!

Adversity Principle #17

In Comforting Others You Will Comfort Yourself

"Then Job answered and said, I have heard many such things: miserable comforters are ye all..." Job 16:1, 2

In this chapter we are going to see how that by helping others, we help ourselves. I just have to share a humorous story about compassion that gets misdirected. Jon was driving home late one night when he picked up a hitchhiker, compassionately trying to reach out and touch the life of this person. As they rode along he began to be suspicious of his passenger.

Jon then checked to see if his wallet was safe in the pocket of his coat that was on the seat between them, but it wasn't there! So he slammed on the brakes ordered the hitchhiker out and said, "Hand over that wallet immediately!" The frightened hitchhiker handed over the billfold and Jon drove off.

When he arrived home he started telling his wife about the experience she said, "Oh, honey by the way before I forget, Jon did you know that you left your wallet at home this morning?" Ha!

That's really the story of Job's friends; they started off saying they were going to help but, but in fact, ended up being a great hurt to his heart. There are at least 42 amazing life lessons on adversity in the book of Job that we are learning. Eliphaz says, "You're arrogant Job, and you think you're always right. You don't appreciate your friends." Job's answer is simply, "Look, I'm not saying I'm right, I'm just saying at this moment what I need is your encouragement. I need your love and support, not your misinformed sermons!"

In chapter 16 and 17 we find Job's response to Eliphaz, *"Then Job answered and said, I have heard many such things: miserable comforters are ye all"*

(Job 16:1, 2). Everybody's been talking about old Job and he says, in perhaps one of the most famous quotes in all of literature, "...miserable comforters are ye all." He really wasn't bitter, he was just saying in effect, "You guys are *not* helping...at all." Learning how to be a good comforter is a wonderful gift from God. Knowing when to talk and knowing when to be silent, is from God. Job didn't need some *answers* he needed *someone*.

Getting back into the swing of things after your mate dies takes a while, but the process is aided as you see that God's gifting to you is to be used, not buried

Learning to get our comfort from God rather than people is not always an easy lesson. Henry Morrison, the great missionary to Africa, over 100 years ago, was coming home from Africa where he had served for decades. As he stood on the deck of the ship looking toward the port he posed the question to his wife, "I wonder if anyone will remember us? Do you think anyone will remember who we are? Will anybody meet us at the dock?" Also on that ship, unknown to Henry, was President Teddy Roosevelt who had gone to Africa on a hunting trip.

As they came into New York harbor, Morrison stood there on the deck and saw throngs of people welcoming the ship. Bands were blaring. Banners everywhere read, "Welcome home." Henry and his wife got so excited! They went down to their cabin to get their luggage. As they came up on deck however they began to realize that all those people had not come to welcome them, but Teddy Roosevelt.

They went to their hotel that night with heavy hearts. The faithful missionary looked at his wife and said, "I really don't get it, we've been in Africa for 40 years. We have poured our life into ministry and the work of God and yet we come back to America and not one single soul comes to welcomes us."

His godly wife sat down next to Henry, put her comforting hand on his shoulder and said, "Honey, you've forgotten something...we're not home yet!" How true! Real comfort for the Christian comes when you realize who you are here for.

Helping others helps yourself. Getting back into the swing of things after your mate dies takes a while, but the process is aided as you see that God's gifting to you is to be used, not buried. In the Parable of the Talents *(Matthew 25),* Jesus impresses on Christians the importance of not losing opportunities given you. From the time of mankind's creation, each individual has been entrusted with resources of time, skills and material goods to varying degrees. Everything we have comes from God and belongs to Him.

We are responsible for using those resources so that they increase in value. As Christians, we additionally have the most valuable resource of all – the Word of God! If we believe and apply His Word as good stewards and use our time, talents and treasure, we will then be a blessing to others and the value of what we do multiplies. We are accountable to the Lord for the use of His resources. Don't bury those talents in the dirt of grief, but use them to be a blessing to others. After things settle down a bit, slowly look for ways to make your life useful! Because helping others helps you heal as you find your life is useful.

Compassion comes from two words: Com – which means to have something together; and passion – feelings. Some say, "I would love to help but I just don't know what to do." Well, here's what you do, if you don't know how to help, just move into *their* body for a few moments. Move into *their* life for a few moments. Move into *their* minds. Think about issues *they* might be facing in their particular situation.

Ask the Holy Spirit to bring things to mind. It will mean "moving into their skin." For a few moments, move into the skin of that young mother who is carrying a baby; move into the skin of that young father who is trying to make a living; move into the skin of the teenage girl whose heart has been broken; move into the skin of that child and move into the skin of that 80 year-old who has fears and financial needs in her life.

When Elijah was discouraged, what did God do? Did God send him a video series on encouragement?

No, God sent him a meal, a friend and let him sleep for a while! Sometimes that is all somebody needs – something practical and simple. I recall one small gift of compassion given to me as a young pastor that made such a big impression. We were living from penny to penny in southern California. I was still going to college, volunteering almost full-time at the church and working a secular job, trying to make a living. We went to a McDonalds to meet several people from the church, including visiting Evangelist, Tom Williams. As we were walking in, Evangelist Williams drove by in his car and called out with a big voice, "Hey Tim!"

I replied, "Hello Brother Williams, how are you?" Just then he said, "Here you go" and proceeded to throw money out his car window. He then rolled up his window and just drove off! That five-dollar bill lying there on the ground made us feel strangely loved... and I'm sure it did the same for him!

Adversity Principle #18

Grief is Good When it Results In Humility

"I have sewed sackcloth upon my skin, and defiled my horn in the dust. My face is foul with weeping, and on my eyelids is the shadow of death..." Job 16:15, 16

Job told his friends, "I know you think that I'm proud and arrogant, but the truth is, I'm a broken man." We humans are well practiced at putting on a good face and pretending that we don't have any problems. But Job knew that putting on masks would not help. He was hurting so bad that even if he had tried, he couldn't convince anyone of his peace. His life was an open book.

Job wasn't trying to put on any airs. He basically was saying, "My stuff's all gone. I can't brag about anything, I'm as low as I possibly can be, I'm not trying to hide anything, I've repented before God." *"Also now, behold, my witness is in heaven, and my record is on high" (Job 16:19).* Job made a wise and strategic choice here. He knew that when life gets crazy and is off the charts, that's typically when we as humans dig down deep and humble ourselves. Many times I've thought to myself, "At least things can't get any worse than this." But guess what, things got worse! Yes, God has a way of pushing us further than we ever thought we could go. The reason for this is so that we will humble ourselves.

Successful living is about becoming and staying humble

Job's friend Elpihaz didn't get that. Bildad didn't get it and Zophar didn't get it either. They couldn't humble themselves...they were holding onto their misguided folklore that all suffering is bad. Job wisely stated, "If I come across as proud, forgive me. If I sound bitter, forgive me. I'm really not...I'm just hurting. I'm suffering." His heart was seeking to see if he had wronged God. His desire was for God to inform him of what might be wrong. And that's the whole book of Job...it's about the fact of God's silence. But God in His divine wisdom couldn't tell Job...yet.

In the New Testament Paul prayed three times for God to remove a thorn in the flesh, but God didn't answer him in his first request or even the second time. When Daniel prayed for God to send an answer, it was 21 days before the answer came (Dan. 10:13). God didn't give Job an answer immediately either.

God allows some people to go through terrible situations and then of all things, hides His face. He grows silent to some of His choice servants because they are the kind of people that will humble themselves and go deeper. And the more humble and broken we can get before God, the more it triggers the grace and strength of God. Successful living is about becoming and staying humble.

I can't even count how many times I have gone to God and would be talking to Him about something when the Holy Spirit will touch a sore spot in my heart.

Many times have I been on my face talking to God when the Holy Spirit whispers, "YOU'RE the issue Tim. Because you and I can talk, I will work on you. That person won't listen to me, but you will. You're close to me and since you're close to me I can talk to you and now I'm going to tell you what you need to hear." I have noticed that the more that I listen to God and the closer that I get to God, the more humble I have to become. The prophet in Isaiah chapter 6 said, "Woe is me, I'm a man of unclean lips." When he realized his life was not up to God's standards, that's when he saw the Lord high and lifted up!

Grief is good when it leads to humility. Anger laden grief will not bring healing and comfort. Beating your pillow in anguish only intensifies your loss. Humble yourself before the Lord, O saint of God! Admit your pain. Ask forgiveness, especially if there is an unbalanced preoccupation with your lost loved one (been there). Life is not over. Hear what God is saying. Remember that brokenness can bring you closer to God's heart. Jesus was called a "man of sorrows." He was never called a comedian. Release your fears and feelings every morning to a God that understands your passion.

Adversity Principle #19

Life Is A Vale Of Tears

"Mine eye also is dim by reason of sorrow, and all my members are as a shadow" Job 17:7

Life is not a party. I sure wish it was. Job had wept so much he thought he had almost lost his eyesight, *"Mine eye also is dim..." (Job 17:7).* He felt as though he was only a "shadow" of the man he used to be.

One of the most beautiful things about the book of Job is that Job is a type of Christ. The message of Christ is a message of suffering, as is Job. The cross speaks to injustice and suffering. The cross of Christ speaks to pain and poverty. In America, we live with so much. The food waste alone, is astronomical. A study by the USDA says that 31% of available food is not eaten (wasted). What a tragedy when half of the world goes to bed hungry at night. Here in America we have to work out at the gym so we won't get fat! Yet much of the world is suffering from over work and lack of nutrition!

We have a God who is touched by those kind of hurts. We have a Savior who is breakable. That is one of the wonderful things about the Christmas story, it tells us that He became a fragile human – He identified with us as humans. God became a person who could hurt. There is no other faith in the world like Christianity! Every other religion says that there is great big god who can hurt *us*. But the Word of God reminds us that we can hurt *Him.* He identifies with us.

Christ suffered and went to the cross for us. That cross was not some beautiful little piece of finished wood. It was an emblem of suffering. Sorrow characterized Jesus' life. His eyes wept often. Jesus carried the burdens of the world. Jesus was a man of deep heartache. How could He not be?

Job reminded his friends, "Brothers you're acting as though life ought to be about partying with your family and having lots of money. You're imagining that life is about fun things. I'm telling you your life is about heartache and recovery." Truly, life is just one issue after another. This fact should not discourage us however, but rather it should make us run to an understanding and caring Savior even more!

Frank E. Graeff was a Methodist minister who served some leading churches in Philadelphia during the late 1800's. Throughout the area, he was known as the "sunshine minister." Yet, in spite of his outwardly-cheery disposition and winsome personality, Graeff was called by God to go through severe testing experiences in his life.

It was while passing through such a test and experiencing doubt and physical agony, that Mr. Graeff wrote the hymn, *Does Jesus Care?* He turned to the Scriptures for strength! 1 Peter 5:7 became especially meaningful to him during this particular struggle: *"Casting all your care upon Him; for He careth for you.*

Does Jesus Care

Does Jesus care when my heart is pained too deeply for mirth and song - As the burdens press, and the cares distress, And the way grows weary and long?

CHORUS: O yes, He cares - I know He cares! His heart is touched with my grief; When the days are weary, the long nights dreary, I know my Savior cares.

Does Jesus care when my way is dark, with a nameless dread and fear? As the daylight fades into deep night shades, Does He care enough to be near?

Does Jesus care when I've tried and failed, to resist some temptation strong? When for my deep grief I find no relief, Tho my tears flow all the night long?

Does Jesus care when I've said good-bye, to the dearest on earth to me, and my sad heart aches till it nearly breaks- Is it aught to Him? Does He see?

CHORUS: O yes, He cares- I know He cares! His heart is touched with my grief; When the days are weary, the long nights dreary, I know my Savior cares.

Adversity Principle # 20

A Victorious Life Can Be An Encouragement For Others Not To Quit

"Upright men shall be astonied at this, and the innocent shall stir up himself against the hypocrite. The righteous also shall hold on his way, and he that hath clean hands shall be stronger and stronger." Job 17:8, 9

Job tells his friends that contrary to popular opinion, his adversity was not leading others to think less of God but more! He found that those around him were actually becoming encouraged, *"Upright men shall be astonied at this...and he that hath clean hands shall be stronger and stronger" (Job 17:8, 9).* Good people were becoming stronger in their faith as they were seeing Job's patience and faith in God. Job's fighting spirit was helping others face what they were going through.

At the turn of the nineteenth century there was a skilled boxer by the name of James Corbet. This was back in the days when they didn't have any of the safety measures that they have now in the sport of boxing. Boxing back then was terrible, bare-fisted fighting. James, known as an incredible scrapper, said the oft-quoted words, "Fight one more round... When your feet are so tired that you feel like you can hardly shuffle out to the middle of the ring, fight one more round! When your hands are so tired and your arms are so weary you feel like you can't hold them up, fight one more round! When your eyes are nearly swollen shut and your face feels like a punching bag, fight one more round! Because you'll always know this, that those who fight one more round are never whipped!"

Job kept getting up every day and he kept fighting for Christ! In the midst of the suffering and sorrow, he kept on keeping on. Because of his indomitable spirit he became a great encouragement to others. Here we are some four or five thousand years later and here we are still telling the story of Job. Unbelievable!

When we get to heaven someday, brothers and sisters, God is going to look at our hands and ask, "Where are your callouses? I put you on earth to work." I heard a godly Christian once state that when he got to heaven he, "...would not want to reach out to the scarred hands of Jesus with soft hands." Life is about the battle. When we get to heaven Jesus is going to say, "Show me your scars." *"I bear in my body...",* Paul said, *"...the marks and sufferings of Jesus" (Gal. 6:17).*

It takes a *test* to have a *testimony!*

Grieving Christians more than at any other time, can become a pacesetter for God. Finding the strength of God to carry on despite your pain, will influence others! Anybody can be joyful when all is going well, but modeling Christian virtues, virtues of true spirituality, when you are hurting is crucial to effective ministry in the world.

One's true spirituality, or godliness (or lack thereof) is revealed in their actions and those actions will of necessity, influence others either for good or for evil. Students, sons, daughters, and the flock, tend to emulate their teachers, parents, or spiritual leaders. The tendency is for us to shy away from responsibility. But in order to help others, we must accept this as a reality of leadership.

Someone is going to follow us and be influenced by us. Are we providing the kind of example that will enhance their lives? We don't need to have everything figured out and put into nice little boxes before we can be used of God. We just need to keep putting one foot in front of the other (and fight one more round!).

God seems to delight in using people with sanctified deficiencies. Consider Jesus and His choice of disciples. How would you like to keep a worldwide campaign going after your death with the good, the bad and the ugly like these guys? Yet, with those common, average, uneducated and yes – broken men, the Lord launched a campaign that has spanned the globe. Was this because of their unique and imaginative methodology? No! It was because those common men knew the Lord and experienced life's challenges in the power of Christ!

Because of the power of our example, we will either negatively or positively influence others. The Scripture repeatedly addresses this responsibility. Christians are to be models for others to imitate. We are to be a picture of reality, a proof that the blood of Jesus Christ saves anyone. Job's life became a powerful magnet that drew others to God. Let's let our lives that have been broken and restored do the same. It takes a *test* to have a *test*imony!

Adversity Principle #21

Don't Expect People To Understand Your Hurt

"He hath put my brethren far from me, and mine acquaintance are verily estranged from me." Job 19:13

Wouldn't it be wonderful if there were always someone there for us in our tough times? Someone who always understood how we were feeling? And there are many that do try and help. But people are fickle and so human in their attempts.

Consider Job's disappointing reality with his family and friends. It's true that it was Satan who prompted everybody's response, but they still had the opportunity to say no, *"My kinsfolk have failed, and my familiar friends have forgotten me. They that dwell in mine house, and my maids, count me for a stranger:*

I am an alien in their sight" (Job 19:14,15). When Job had his beautiful home, when he had money, when he had the resources, when he had the beautiful family, everybody hung out with Job. But, when he lost it they all turned away!

So uncertain is the friendship of our fellow humans... so changeable, *"I called my servant, and he gave me no answer; I intreated him with my mouth" (Job 19:16).* The same ones who used to say, "You're the best boss", wouldn't even talk to him now. He had been a good employer, but now when he asked for them to come, they turned on him. It is true, Job might have been a bit hypersensitive in his recollections (it is common when you're going through real times of suffering to feel like everybody's against you). But in this case, we see that everybody really *had* pulled back. Job even begged them for help and still they kept their distance.

If that wasn't bad enough, consider this (this is something that is hard for me to imagine), *"My breath is strange to my wife, though I intreated for the children's sake of mine own body" Job (19:17).* His wife had drawn away, so much so that she did not even want to get close to him! "My breath is strange", is a poetic and sad way of saying that she would not even come close enough to kiss him anymore. You might imagine his enemies rejoicing that he was down. You might even imagine that his business competitors might've been happy at his trouble. It's even thinkable how some employees might've turned their back on him and maybe even some extended family members. In the end, the devil prompted Job's wife to stick in the most terrible dagger of all, because she stabbed him in the heart when she turned her back on God.

We can't justify her actions but can honestly understand that she was deeply hurt as well. Notice Job's pathetic and pleading statement, *"...I intreated for the children's sake of mine own body" (Job 19:17).* He said, "At least for the children's sake couldn't we have a togetherness here? For the children's sake couldn't we somehow make this work, somehow get this back together?"

He then exclaimed how hurt he was by the mocking of the local children, *"Yea, young children despised me; I arose, and they spake against me" (Job 19:18).* And if that wasn't hard enough, *"All my inward friends abhorred me: and **they whom I loved** are turned against me" (Job 19:19).* All of his closest friends turned on him. He lost his possessions. He lost his children. He lost his business. He lost his health. He lost his kinfolk.

It wasn't like Job was a mean guy. It wasn't like he was some kind of terrible person that got what he deserved. This was a deeply loving man. This was a man who cared about his friends. It doesn't say that he just cared for them it says that he *loved* them and yet they all turned away.

As I read these verses I weep! I grieve for Job. I hurt for Job. Then I think about Christ. There He was on the cross…my Savior. The one who gave His life, the one who gave His all. He loved me and I turned my back on Him. Everybody turned their back on Christ. Peter turned his back on Him. And John turned his back on Him. And James turned his back on Him. Every human turned their back on Jesus! Each one, one by one, stood back as He was on the cross hanging between heaven and earth all by himself. He bore *all* the shame, He took *all* the heartache.

We see in Job, a Savior. His friends didn't get it, they were on a theological merry-go-round. They were jabbering while Job was dying and suffering. He was as low as a person could get and they were playing games with words.

You will have to give God all your expectations concerning the people in your life. Only God will always be there

I have spent a good deal of time relating Job's dire situation so that you can identify with him about the frailties of humanity. You will have to give God all your expectations concerning the people in your life. Only God will always be there. Frankly, people will say stupid and hurtful things without even realizing it. People will tell you things that aren't true about your grief. Death brings out the best and the worst in people, so be prepared. People will tell you what you should and shouldn't feel and how you should and shouldn't grieve. For the most part just avoid negative people. Despite what they think is good, most *people don't understand* how to help and support you…but God always does and will!

Adversity Principle #22

Strength Is Received By Confessing The Word

"For I know that my redeemer liveth, and that he shall stand at the latter day upon the earth: And though after my skin worms destroy this body, yet in my flesh shall I see God" Job 19:25, 26

In the midst of everything Job is going through, he finds the presence of mind to make a confession of his faith. He basically says to his friends (and family), "You all can continue to say what you want to…you children can laugh but, this is something I know that I know that I know that I know – a better day *is* coming!"

Job didn't have anything else to hang onto. He didn't have the pleasure of waking up, going out and looking at his fields. He had no fields. He could not look forward to going out and butchering livestock and having a party. He had no cows and no family for a party. There was nothing he had to hold onto anymore. But there was one thing that he did have! There was one thing that he had not lost. There was one thing that was down in the deepest part of his soul. He had a Redeemer that was alive. He had a *personal* savior. He had a personal *living* Savior!

Some might be reading this and say, "There must be some mistake, Jesus hadn't even been born yet. He hadn't died and risen yet...how could He be Job's Savior?" This is all true. It would be some 3000 years before Christ would be born, live a perfect life, be crucified at the hands of sinful man and then rise from the dead. But here is how that works. Those that lived in the Old Testament looked ahead to Christ and those of us who live in this New Testament era, look back to Christ. Jesus is called the lamb that was slain from the foundation of the earth (Rev. 13:8).

I love Job's statement in 19:26, *"And though after my skin worms destroy this body, yet in my flesh shall I see God..."* He knew from scripture that even if his body were to be destroyed, God would take the dust particles that were in a million places in the universe, gather them back together and reunite his body. Hallelujah! What an awesome privilege to be a believer! Someday the trumpet will sound and the dead in Christ will rise with the same body, albeit ever new. Job kept himself encouraged by confessing the Word.

You can see a climax in the book of Job in this chapter. There is a real apex here. From this point forward and in the balance of the book, we don't see Job being quite so grouchy in his emotions. It is as though something happened here at this moment. I believe it was the wonderful outpouring of the Spirit. It was at the moment when his confession began to ring out.

Friend, we live in a negative world. These negative influences are evident at every turn. If it's not the doom and gloom of the news, it's one candidate running for office bashing the other. When you add grief into that and the pressures of the world it will, if allowed, steal the love and joy from your life.

So, how do we stay positive in a negative world? Let me give an example. In 1 Samuel, we read the story of a terrible situation that David was facing. His father-in-law, Saul, was trying to kill him. He had been running for his life every day for several years. His possessions had been burned, his family had been taken, and his own men wanted to stone him. Yet it says in *1 Samuel 30:6, "And David was greatly distressed; for the people spake of stoning him, because the soul of all the people was grieved, every man for his sons and for his daughters: but David encouraged himself in the Lord his God."* Things looked bleak.

David was in a situation where everything seemed bad, but David *encouraged himself* in the Lord. How? I believe he took the Word and began to speak it to himself, and then it was only a matter of hours or days until there was a turnaround. If he had given in at that last minute, he would have lost.

I often see people, myself included, who have been hurt deeply, start listening to the evil one. Satan wins the battle for the mind when they don't have a battle plan. It's been said often, "If you don't stand for something you will fall for anything"! You might ask, "How long will it take until I get passed this?" Here is what you do - you speak the Word of God and His promises until you're encouraged. Don't quit! I found that studying, witnessing, preaching and sharing the word of God – as opportunity arose – helped give me a feeling that I was needed and life was not over after Lynette died.

You need to recognize that Satan is using the evil and negative things of this world to discourage you. If you don't resist this, it will cause you to be discouraged. The Bible says in *Isaiah 26:3* that the Lord will, *"keep him in perfect peace."* When does peace happen? When our mind is "stayed" (focused) on God. How do we keep our eyes on Jesus? One of the best ways is to – out loud – speak forth the Word. Our peace is linked directly to what we think. What we think is directly linked to what we speak. Listen friend, unless you have a deliberate plan to encourage yourself in the Lord, it will not happen. Praise God... you can do this! Speak the Word!

Adversity Principle #23

Only God Can Figure Things Out

"As for me, is my complaint to man? and if it were so, why should not my spirit be troubled?" Job 21:4

Pain is something that we all go through at some point. Sometimes I think to myself when adversity hits, "For which of the one thousand things that I've done, is it that I am now suffering?" It is true, sometimes we *do* bring consequences upon ourselves. We run a red light, and then bemoan our tough time when the ticket comes. We fudge on our taxes and suffer loss of income as we pay penalties. We neglect our teeth and find out we have cavities. The truth is, a lot of our pain really is self-inflicted. However, there are many times when loss has no human rhyme or reason to it.

In a single day Job's good life was devastated. All of his earthly possessions were stripped away. Ten beautiful children all killed in a violent windstorm. Job then loses his health. So there he sat, broken and penniless outside the walls of the city among the "unclean" outcasts. In such a situation you would think that people would come and extend their pity, but it was soon evident that the devil was at work among his friends. At a moment like this it would be easy to let go of God. But Job held onto his faith with a godly stubbornness.

We can know this – every life is a complete life

When I was growing up, children would chant on the schoolyard, "cheaters never prosper." But as I've grown up, I've found out that's actually not true. In fact, cheaters often do prosper. Generally speaking, evil people do suffer, but that's not an ironclad fact. For example, the press will ask a person who has turned a hundred years old what the secret has been to living so long and some old grizzly guy will say, "It's because I always drank whiskey!" Obviously it's not always people who abuse their lives and bodies that die early. David Brainerd was one of the great prayer warriors of the faith. He was mightily used of God as a missionary in the 1700's among the native American, yet he died at the early age of twenty-nine! God is in charge.

Job reminded his friend, "I don't stand or fall because of man... God is in charge." Job knew that if his success was based merely on what people had to say he was in big trouble. But he knew he would stand before God as judge. Job went on to remind us all, *"Mark me, and be astonished, and lay your hand upon your mouth" (Job 21:5).* Job rightly states that the best thing for people to do, rather than just spouting out off-key theology, was to put their hand over their mouth, i.e. think twice about what you say! Everybody, ourselves included, need to take a step back at times and say, "God knows what He is doing even if nobody else does!"

This ancient word of wisdom is great advice to our current generation too. Hush up! The loss of a loved one often prompts the question, "Where was God when my child (husband, wife, etc.) died?" We can know this – *every* life is a complete life. That means God knows exactly how long each of us will live. Its length is "appointed" by God (Hebrews 9:27). Some miscarry; some live more than a century. But every life is a complete life. We may not understand this Bible truth in its entirety, but embracing it can help. God makes no mistakes.

God has purposes that we cannot understand. I have a difficult time trying to stay on top of my own life and schedule, so I should not be surprised then that the One who created the universe and keeps all of it running, thinks and acts in ways I can't begin to understand. Some things are beyond our understanding, *"The secret things belong to the LORD our God..." (Deuteronomy 29:29a).* I admit it's terribly hard to understand why God would take one whom we love so much and who we feel had so much left to give.

Right now, at this moment, none of us can fully understand why. But I'm convinced that in heaven we will understand. Death happens to all humans. We all are part of the fallen human race that has a death sentence attached. C.S. Lewis once said, "Wars don't cause death. Wars simply hurry the process for some people." All of us will die; it's just a question of when. One day, thank God that will change! But for now, we push forward day-by-day in a world of birthing and dying.

The timing of death is perplexing to say the least. But I can never forget that the most unfair death of all was that of Jesus Christ. Although God called Jesus His "beloved Son" (Mathew 3:17), His life was taken that we might gain eternal life. Jesus's death was not "fair" in any usual sense of the term, yet He freely gave His life for us. It is Christ's "unfair" death that gives us the great hope we have today!

Adversity Principle #24

Learn To Let Go And Let God

"They spend their days in wealth, and in a moment go down to the grave. Shall any teach God knowledge? seeing he judgeth those that are high." Job 21:13, 22

To be sure, God has His own time agenda. God determines for one to go to the grave early and for another to live a long life. A person's length of life doesn't reflect God's love or displeasure for that individual. He loves everybody (John 3:16). God's ways and judgment are far above ours. It is *God's* business if He wants to shorten a man's life or lengthen it. We need to let go and let God be God.

Job's "friends" point out (at least it is very obvious to them), that Job must be an evil person. All you have to do is look at his troubles. These friends also feel it is their responsibility to make a public declaration of their opinions. They think they are on a mission from God. They will dig up dirt until they find evidence of his "true" nature.

Job had had a number of servants (employees). These character assassins ("friends") go on a search and find a disgruntled employee here and there. Of course, you're surely going to find some servant who didn't like what Job did at one time, *"Thou hast not given water to the weary to drink, and thou hast withholden bread from the hungry" (Job 22:7).* An "uncaring boss" was the title leveled at him.

Had Eliphaz heard some juicy story? Well, whatever he felt or thought he saw, this is NOT the time to do it. You can count on this though – people can and will say just about anything about anybody's life regardless of how factual it is. It makes absolutely no difference what you do in life, you *will* be criticized. I ask myself as I read Eliphaz's complaint, "What were you trying to accomplish? What good were you doing? Who did you think you were helping by spreading all those innuendos?" The truth was, his outright lies and misspeaking did far more harm than whatever he was accusing Job of!

I let the tears flow, because I have come to realize they are a sign that I am surrendering to God the reality of my loss

My goal in bringing up this scenario is to point out the unnecessary emotional grief that we often cause ourselves when we try to tell God what to do. You and I need to "let Go and let God!" Loss involves change, and most of us don't do change very well. When you cherish something, you hold on to it... and hold we do! So when it is stripped from us by circumstances, there is pain. We'd like to let go of the pain, but sometimes we just can't. Fruit falls from the tree only when it is mature. Such is the way of letting hurts go. God has His own timing as it relates to the circumstances of my life.

The key here is to keep growing and maturing through time in the Word of God, meditation on His nature and heartfelt prayer walks with Jesus. Then, supernaturally, when the inner man gets mature, the hurts of the past begin to drop away. This is not to say the process is painless. It's not. But there is a power that comes as we let go to God.

That was my experience when I realized it was time to stop wearing my wedding ring and start cleaning out my wife's side of the closet. I felt a deep sadness and yet a submitting to God. There was a "rightness" to it – to moving on. As the months passed, the deep feelings of the past were not so acute as they once were. Of course, I had my tough times (and still do). And when those feelings arise. I let the tears flow, because I have come to realize they are a sign that I am surrendering to God the reality of my loss. Don't try and teach God what to do. Just let go and let God!

Adversity Principle #25

God Understands

"Oh that I knew where I might find ***him****! that I might come even to his seat! I would order my cause before him, and fill my mouth with arguments. I would know the words which he would answer me, and understand what he would say unto me." Job 23:3-5*

We notice that Job had it right, he wasn't trying to find an *it* in his troubles, he was trying to find *Him!* Years ago, in the 1970's, there was a nationwide evangelistic program named, "I Found It." It was a well-meaning campaign that did some good. But there was a strange feeling that welled up inside of me every time I saw those words "I found IT." Jesus is a person, not a feeling or an "it." Job knew that he had a personal Savior and that someday in heaven he would get all the facts!

Let's look, for just a moment, at a so-called "contradiction" in the Bible. Does God judge people who have sinful lives? Yes. Does He bring sickness and loss of finances? Yes, *"Fools because of their transgression, and because of their iniquities, are afflicted" (Psalm 107:17).* But while people suffer because of sin, there is another verse that states, *"Many are the afflictions of the righteous: but the LORD delivereth him out of them all" (Psalm 34:19).*

What? Wait a second, didn't we just read that sinners because of their iniquities are afflicted? Then which is true? Do these verses contradict each other?

Not at all, they are "balancing truths." Even secular philosophy understands balancing truth's. How about this one, "Look before you leap." Is this true? Most of the time it is. What about this quote, "He who hesitates is lost." Is that true? Yes, that's actually true most of the time. If we have a really great opportunity that we neglect to take advantage of out of fear, we may lose that chance forever. Are both true? Yes. It is true that we should take opportunities and it is equally true that we should be cautious.

And the same thing is true about the wicked people suffering and the righteous suffering; which is true? They're both true. Is Jesus full of grace? Absolutely. But is He full of truth? Oh yes...for sure. Is salvation by faith or works? Faith, but God wants us at the same time to work because we've *been* saved. There are many such balancing truths in scripture. God directs His people to proceed with discernment.

Tears release the pain we cannot put into words

Job was simply saying that there are *some* facts that we'll not be able to really gain an understanding of until we get to see Him in glory. Understanding how life at times can be both so joyous and so sad, is difficult. Grief is an emotion common to the human experience. Many Bible characters experienced deep loss and sadness. Even Jesus wept for His friends, Mary and Martha (John 11). After Lazarus died, Jesus went to the village of Bethany, where Lazarus was buried. When Jesus saw Mary and Martha (Lazarus's sisters) weeping, He also wept. He was moved by their grief. He understood. He is a sympathetic High Priest (Hebrews 4:15).

God cares about every tear of grief you cry. Scripture tells us to weep with those who weep. Tears release the pain we cannot put into words. In the moments when you feel most alone, God is present with you in your grief. Our tears are a language all their own; a language, that for the believer, only the Holy Spirit truly understands (Romans 8:26). That means that God hears and understands what your heart is saying in the midst of tears. I often say that my favorite prayer promise is "O." Have you ever noticed how often an author in Psalms starts off a verse of prayer to God with just a groan – "O"! There are no great theological truths there...just a divine groan.

Do you ever wonder if God really understands what is happening in your life? Does He hear your cries? Does He see your tears? Does He care? Yes He does! Consider God's people that were slaves in Egypt. God had not forgotten them (Ex. 3:7). God says, "I have seen...I have heard...I know." Yes, God understands. He will do the same for you. Dr. Oswald Smith, Canadian Pastor and Author wrote –

God understands your sorrows, He sees the falling tear; And whispers, 'I am with thee," Then falter not, nor fear.

God understands your heartaches, He knows the bitter pain; O, trust Him in the darkness, You cannot trust in vain.

God understands your weakness, He knows the tempter's power; And He will walk beside you however dark the hour. He understands your longing, your deepest grief He shares; then let Him bear your burden, He understands and cares!

Adversity Principle #26

Adversity Is A Refining Fire For Our Good

"But he knoweth the way that I take: when he hath tried me, I shall come forth as gold." Job 23:10

Job got it. He finally began to get some perspective through all the adversity. Job exclaimed, "I see God's hand is in this. I see God's fingerprints everywhere." Now, does that sound like a nervous wreck? No, this is a man of faith. In the midst of his sorrow, suffering, pain, incredible heartache and confusion he says, "I *know* this much– I *shall* come forth as gold! God is not throwing me away. He's throwing me into a refining fire."

There's a big difference between throwing something into a trashcan to get rid of it, and putting something into a fire to cure it. It comes down to the fact that the hotter the furnace the better the gold; the more the heat, the more highly refined and valuable the finished product will be.

In the midst of incredible heartache and with suffering flowing over him like a river he said, "I can see the hand of God." He didn't like it. He wept over it. He was grouchy and testy at times. He wanted to die. Yet...in the midst of it all he knew by faith, that God had a plan. Job proclaimed, "He's my redeemer and I know He's got a plan for my life." Now that's faith! Not just some old, cold stark creed. No, Job had a *personal* Savior.

The metaphor is meant to help us understand the purpose behind the pain – to conform us to the character of Christ

The year was 1818 and the country was France. There was a little boy of nine by the name of Luis who was in his father's workshop, a harness maker by trade. The boy loved to watch his father make the beautiful leatherwork. He said to his dad, "Someday father, I want to be a harness maker just like you." His dad replied, "Son, why not start right now?"

He walked over to the table, got a piece of hide and gave his son a sharp woodworking tool and hammer. He said, "Here, be careful now. Hammer here and over here." The boy took the hammer and struck the tool. But the tip broke! It then bounced off the hard table and struck his eye, blinding it! Not many months later his other eye tragically lost sight. Here was this boy, now blind, who had to spend the rest of his life without sight.

Someone came by his house and as he was sitting there, handed him a pinecone to hold. As he was feeling the pinecone, with his now very tender hands rubbing over it, an idea came to his mind, "Perhaps I can put some marks on paper so that people who are blind can feel them and actually learn to read on their own." So he made an alphabet out of little raised dots on paper. Luis Braille came up with the Brail tactile learning system so that people who were blind could read. The fire of testing that he had to go through became the basis of a blessing for so many people.

The word picture Job uses about being "refined" is a colorful and profound picture. There are quite a few references to the refining of gold and silver in scripture. The metaphor is meant to help us understand the purpose behind the pain—to conform us to the character of Christ. Character is forged over time, especially in the tough times. God is the Refiner.

Notice these steps in the refining process:

The Breaking

In Biblical times, a refiner began by breaking up rough ore so the valuable metal could be exposed to the heat. Adversity opens up the sin hardened places of our lives.

The Placing

The refiner then puts broken ore into a "crucible"—a fireproof melting pot. The refiner places the crucible into the furnace at the precise temperature necessary for removing other metals that would mar the quality of the precious metal. Few events in life are a better crucible for shaping character than loss.

The Heating

As the ore melts in the crucible under the watchful eye of the refiner, a layer of impurities called "dross" eventually forms on the surface that is then skimmed off. For us individually, dross represents anything that keeps us from being all that God wants us to be.

The Purifying

The refiner turns up the heat and places the crucible back into the furnace to really get the job done. He knows that certain impurities will only be released at certain temperatures. Life is often a fire. Grief comes when God turns up the heat in our lives.

The Reflecting

With utmost skill and patience, the refiner removes the dross, leaving behind gleaming metal...more pure and precious than before. Only when the refiner sees a clear reflection of himself is the process complete. Finally, the precious metal attains its highest degree of purity!

And that, my friend, describes God's loving intentions for allowing us to be in the fire. Trust Him to use your trial for good. Let God give you eyes to see the "silver lining." How do we hang on to hope in the midst of lonely times? We persevere by trusting the heart of the One who allowed the trial...trusting in His perfect plan and His justice.

Adversity Principle #27

Plow On

"Neither have I gone back from the commandment of his lips; I have esteemed the words of his mouth more than my necessary food." Job 23:12

I borrow the title of this principle from my good friend Evangelist Paul Tsika. He reminded me often to just keep on keeping on! Despite whatever adversities we encounter as we obey the Word, we must carry on. Job kept pressing on. His trial didn't drive him *from* God, his trial drove him *to* God.

And that's how you can know where your heart is. In the midst of your suffering and heartache where do you go? Do you run to a bottle? Do you run to the pills? Do you run to something fleshly to ease the pain? Do you quit church, stop praying or forget to read your Bible because you're upset? Or does suffering drive us closer to God? I love the wonderful quote by Charles Spurgeon, "Good men are washed towards God by the rough waves of their grief!" Amen and amen! When a godly Christian's sorrows are deepest, their highest desire is not to escape from God but to escape to God.

Their heart proclaims: If God has humbled me, let's make good use of it. If God's plan is to hurt me, then let's make good use of it. Let's get closer to God in the midst of this incredible trial. Let's not waste this suffering. If I'm going to have to go through this junk, then at least let me get closer to God. I can live without my fun and I can even live without food for awhile if I have to, but I cannot live without my Bible!

That's what Job affirmed, as he said, "I have esteemed the commandments of God, the rules of God more beautiful and more precious than my necessary food. I'll give up anything but I won't give up my Bible." In fact, the word "esteem" in the Hebrew is to lay it up, to hide it, to hide it in a place so I will have it when I come back.

Martin Luther, the fearless reformer was asked as he stood before a council, "Where will you be when all of your supporters desert you?" He replied, "I will be where I've always been, in the hands of a sovereign God." Where will you be, Job, when you lose all of your money, your business and your family? "I will be where I've always been, in the hands of a loving God. It's true, I can't always figure God out. Life is not fun right now. I'm going through a terrible time of suffering, but I will tell you one thing; my God is a good and loving God and I will plow on."

Adversity Principle #28

Someday We Will Know Why God Does What He Does

"Why, seeing times are not hidden from the Almighty, do they that know him not see his days?" Job 24:1

Our lives are not hidden from God. He knows your "times." That is, your past is not hidden from His judgment. Your present is not hidden from His eye. Your future is not hidden from His knowledge. God is aware and governs every facet of our times.

I believe that there's a day coming in which the God that we serve, is going to give us a true understanding of what's happening in our lives. Won't that be a great day? Amen to that! God does not make "bad" things to happen in life. Rather, "bad" things happen within the freedom that comes with the gift of life. Any "bad" thing which happens, is never the last word however. Rather, God has the deepest and last word!

Job brings up some very human questions; questions that often trouble humanity. For example, Job points out the terrible mistreatment, at times, of the fatherless, *"They pluck the fatherless from the breast, and take a pledge of the poor" (Job 24:9).* Other examples of human tragedy that Job alerts us to are murder (24:14) and sexual sin (24:15). I think it is an amazing quality of Job that in the midst of all his suffering he could say, "I'm not the only one that's hurting here. The poor are being mistreated. Families are being destroyed. There is much blight in our society. I'm not the only one that's having a tough time." Job is to be commended for seeing all that was going on even during his own trials.

God does not make "bad" things happen in life. Rather "bad" things happen in the freedom that comes with the gift of life

Despite his grief, Job persisted in believing the truth

about the realities of life. It is just not meant for us to understand every detail of life. Just know that He loves you. And *someday*—if not in this life, then in the life to come—you will understand how God can take even the most unspeakable losses and turn them to joy. Even though you do not understand your own adversity, pain and grief – someday He will unveil His perfect wisdom in eternity! Someday, believe it or not, you will no longer want to hold on to the pain. Gradually you will get light.

Perhaps the old Hymn, *Someday He'll Make It Plain*, by Lida Leech says it best,

I do not know why oft 'round me
My hopes all shattered seem to be;
God's perfect plan I cannot see,
But someday I'll understand.

Refrain:
Someday He'll make it plain to me,
Someday when I His face shall see;
Someday from tears I shall be free,
For someday I shall understand.

I cannot tell the depth of love,

Which moves the Father's heart above;

My faith to test, my love to prove,

But someday I'll understand.

Though trials come through passing days,

My life will still be filled with praise;

For God will lead through darkened ways,

But someday I'll understand

Adversity Principle #29

People Talk Too Much

"How hast thou counselled him that hath no wisdom? and how hast thou plentifully declared the thing as it is? To whom hast thou uttered words? and whose spirit came from thee?" Job 26:3, 4

In the New Testament book of James, we're told to look at the life of Job for a good example of how to respond to adversity. I am glad God takes precious space in scripture to show us how to respond to tough times. The only believers, that I am aware of, that don't have any troubles are gathered in little neighborhoods in communities all across our land – places we call cemeteries! These are the only humans who will never suffer again.

Now, it's true that some of our troubles are all in our head. Mark Twain said, "There has been much tragedy in my life and at least half of it actually happened." On other occasions we bring hard times upon ourselves - life becomes like a train wreck. It just goes from one crazy thing to the next.

Job is grieved, broken and hurting. What he needed was the mercy and grace of God. But sadly what he got from the people around him was verbiage without end. Job exclaims facetiously, "You're the smartest people that have ever lived…I got it. And I get how great God is. I'm not going to argue with you about that. Our God *is* a sovereign and amazing God. But my hope and prayer is that you would support me and pray for me during this time; you're talking so much that I can't see God."

How do you wade through the sea of words that swirl in times of heartache? Be grateful for friends who, with a minimum of words, simply acknowledge and accept the fact that you are grieving without trying to analyze it. But if they do try to interpret your grief, try to gracefully accept their gesture even if it is not particularly helpful. It will likely be less of a hassle if you just hear them out and move on.

When it's your turn to help, do so by reaching out thoughtfully. Communicate your caring mostly with gestures such as gift cards, money and acts of service. Acknowledge the fact that they are hurting and pray for them. Most people who are grieving want, and need, little more than to know that their friends are close by, waiting with them and paying attention to them as they go through a difficult time. The fact is, grief is a problem that no one can "fix", you just get "through" it.

Adversity Principle #30

Creation Reminds Us That God's Ways Are Past Finding Out

"He stretcheth out the north over the empty place, and hangeth the earth upon nothing" Job 26:7

If we look around, we will see that creation teaches us to take a step back and see God as one who has a plan that is beyond our "pay scale." God is a whole lot bigger than we think He is, *"He stretched out the north over the empty place, and hangeth the earth upon nothing" (Job 26:7).* Ancient Greek scientists said the earth was resting on the shoulders of Atlas! Had they read the Bible, they would have seen that God was "hanging the world on nothing." That is, the laws of gravitation where at work, not mythological gods. This earth hangs on nothing. That is, it's spinning in it's own orbit. Now, I can't even hang Christmas tree lights without having issues let alone "hanging" all the planets. My point is that taking a good look at God's wisdom in creation may help reset your spirit. Maybe a good walk on the beach might help you to see that God is *way* big!

The difficulties we experience in this life take on new meaning when we see them against the backdrop of creation

Gods ways are past finding out. Even if He told you why things were happening, would you understand? Definitely not. Job asks, "Have you ever wondered why the clouds that are so full of moisture they don't just burst and tear open like a big wet soggy bag?" *"He bindeth up the waters in his thick clouds; and the cloud is not rent under them" (Job 26:8).* The book of Job is the oldest book in the Bible. It was written far before any human had the instruments to understand the scientific facts of meteorology. And yet here Job is talking about the amazing fact that clouds actually are full of moisture and therefore full of weight. For example: carry a gallon of milk around for a while and you will find it is heavy! Does a cloud weigh anything or does it just kind of float around like steam or a vapor? An average cumulous cloud of a cubic kilometer contains millions of gallons of water and actually weighs over two billion pounds! Well, here again God's Word rings true. God holds water in clouds.

God not only made the heavens functional, but beautiful as well, *"By his spirit he hath garnished the heavens; his hand hath formed the crooked serpent" (Job 26:13).* God loves beautiful things. He paints incredible sunsets. We serve a Creator who is the Father of lights, *"Lo, these are parts of his ways: but how little a portion is heard of him? But the thunder of his power who can understand?" (Job 26:14).* Job reminds us that the heavens are only a part of the glory of God. If you think that you've got God all figured out, you don't even have a clue.

The difficulties we experience in this life take on new meaning when we see them against the backdrop of creation. Hard times are a way through which God works to accomplish His will in our lives. When we are in trouble we see that pressures that are too big for us, are not for a big God that keeps the stars in place. In this way, God gets our attention. We are told in Romans chapter 1 that the heavens declare the glory of God.

In hard times we can't continue to do life status quo. We have to ask God for wisdom, obey His Word, and then trust Him to bring the help we need. Emotions, like intense grief, point out our weaknesses and prompt us to rely on a big God in ways that we wouldn't unless we had needs. On our own we can't live in a way that honors God. We need to rely on God and receive His grace.

Adversity Principle #31

Don't Let Self-Reproach Weigh You Down

"God forbid that I should justify you: till I die I will not remove mine integrity from me. My righteousness I hold fast, and will not let it go: my heart shall not reproach me so long as I live." Job 27:5,6

Now we're going to see Job boldly speak a great truth to his own defense. Unfortunately, his "friends" have pushed him and pushed and finally he has to speak up. His life is in turmoil and yet he has to defend his faith in God.

He gets a little bit forceful, but notice the power behind the words, *"As God liveth, who hath taken away my judgment; and the Almighty, who hath vexed my soul; All the while my breath is in me and the spirit of God is in my nostrils; My lips shall not speak wickedness, nor my tongue utter deceit" (Job 27:2-4).* He basically states he knows that while he is not perfect, the spirit of God was in him (in his nostrils). He knew he was a saved man. He also has to remind them that he was a man of integrity, *"God forbid that I should justify you: till I die I will not remove mine integrity from me. My righteousness I hold fast, and will not let it go: my heart shall not reproach me so long as I live" (Job 27:5-6).* That, my friend, is a tremendous principle for getting through adversity. Too many that are grieving suffer from self-reproach.

After the death of a loved one people often express regrets. There are things we wish we had done or said. There might be a widow who had planned on doing extensive traveling with her husband after he retired from work and then was unable to fulfill her dream as he was suddenly diagnosed with a terminal illness. You may regret not being with your Dad at the time of his death. Perhaps you regret expressing frustration at the amount of care your loved one needed, or wish you had expressed your love and telling them how much you would miss him.

For the most part these are feelings we have because we are human and not because of bad morals. But the devil is sure to plant seeds of false guilt whenever he can. Filling your mind and spirit constantly with the Word of God will help stave off self-reproach.

Viktor E. Frankl survived horrendous experiences in Nazi concentration camps. His book, *Man's Search for Meaning*, was written after his release and became an international best seller. Viktor Frankl sums up how they were able to keep going even as they were being told they were trash. He said a person can have everything taken away except for their freedom, "to choose one's attitude in any given set of circumstances, to choose one's own way."

Maybe you are mourning the death of a very special person. You too may wonder how you will get up in the morning. Satan, who is called the Accuser of the Brethren, will bring up many regrets. You have to choose how you will respond. You cannot change the fact the person has died. You cannot go back and do things for them now. What you can do is to choose to move ahead in your walk with God.

Job was not sinless. He knew that he had many failures, but he would not let it be said that somehow he didn't have a love for God. I love what Abraham Lincoln once said, "I never had a policy; I just tried to do my best every day." The best thing we can do to avoid self-reproach after the death of someone we love, is to do the right thing. When you do the "next right thing", as Elizabeth Eliot says, your heart will be strengthened.

The apostle Paul said it this way, *"Herein do I exercise myself daily to be void of offence towards God and towards man" (Acts 24:16).* The way to strengthen your prayers before God is to come to Him in your integrity. This isn't perfection, just sincerity. Of course, there will be some people that you can never please.

The story is told of an old man whose grandson rode the donkey while he walked. As they were travelling from one city to another the old man heard some people mumbling, "Would you look at that old man walking, suffering on his feet while that strong young boy is totally capable of walking." The criticism cut deep so he changed positions. The man started riding the donkey while the boy walked. But sure enough others started grumbling, "Would you look at that a healthy strong man riding the donkey and making that little boy suffer, can you believe that?" So the man, in order to avoid criticism changed again, this time he and the boy both hopped on the donkey and they started riding. Well you guessed it...people *still* criticized him! He could hear people saying, "Would you look at those big people making that poor donkey suffer." So he and his grandson both jumped down and started walking, thinking no one could possibly criticize them now. But, soon he heard people saying, "Would you look at that, they are wasting a perfectly good donkey." The old man was at wits end on what to do. So the man...decided to carry the donkey and the boy!"

The devil will bring accusation to vex your soul regardless of what you have done or not done in life.

But you can take away his ammunition by living with a clear conscience. Job knew that if you're a hypocrite there is no place to find peace and hope, *"For what is the hope of the hypocrite, though he hath gained, when God taketh away his soul?" (Job 27:8).* I can tell you that many times over the years, I've had to check and recheck my motives. I have had to ask myself, "Why am I doing what I am doing?" Satan is an expert at getting us confused through reproachful accusation. Do right as best you can. Give your regrets to the Lord through prayer and then move forward. Don't let self-reproach dismantle your future.

Adversity Principle #32

God Settles Matters In His Time

"This is the portion of a wicked man with God, and the heritage of oppressors, which they shall receive of the Almighty." Job 27:13

In the midst of all the heartache that Job had to endure, he stubbornly held to the fact that while God Almighty's justice does not always fall quickly, it is sure to come. The circumstances surrounding your loved one's death may not seem fair, but you can reassure yourself that God is always loving and just.

The process of faith in God's justice is often complex and very personal. In *A Grief Observed,* C.S. Lewis chronicled his painful struggle with grief and anger at God after his beloved wife died of cancer. Lewis, a well-known writer and theologian, was tormented by questions of God's fairness. He wrote with honesty about the desperation and painful doubts he felt. Here is an example of his feelings about God during this time:

"...go *to Him when your need is desperate...and what do you find? A door slammed in your face...and after that, silence...The longer you wait, the more emphatic the silence becomes..."*

When we hurt, we want to hold someone accountable for our torment. If a person is to blame for our loved one's death, as with drunk driving or murder, we think we have an obvious focus for our anger. But the fact is, only an "Almighty" God can truly hold oppressors accountable. You may have a feeling of frustration, even anger directed at the deceased for dying. We may also shift our anger to anyone in close proximity: doctors, nurses, friends, other relatives and even strangers are all open to our bitter grumbling.

The question lingers: "Is God fair?" Fortunately for

us, God is not fair! Fairness, as defined commonly, would mean that everyone receives exactly the same treatment in life. If that definition were true then if God was completely fair, we would all spend eternity in hell paying for our sin! That is certainly what we all deserve. We have all sinned against God *(Romans 3:23)* and are therefore worthy of eternal death *(Romans 6:23).* No, God is not fair; instead He is just, which is much, much better. Being just He accepted the willing sacrifice of Jesus Christ dying on the cross in our place. Jesus took the punishment that we deserve *(2 Corinthians 5:21).* All we have to do is humbly receive that and we will be saved, forgiven, and we will receive an eternal home in heaven *(John 3:16).*

The fact is, life is not fair. It never has been, and it never will be. Some people are born with advantages; others are born with serious challenges. We constantly hear of bad things happening to innocent people, and of wicked people prospering and seemingly having everything go their way. My wife was a wonderful helper in ministry, mother of nine children and a host of grandchildren. She spent time with Jesus everyday. She was a great blessing to society. Why would God take her? The fact is she was going to die at sometime anyway. God's timing is all His own!

Life is filled with hardships and disappointments. Unfortunately, we struggle with the misconception that life is always supposed to be a "happy experience." We fail to realize however that God's timing and plan is not ours. We can be sure of His just reckoning, but we cannot be sure of the timing.

When we hurt, we want to hold someone accountable for our torment

Jesus made it clear that good times and hard times happen in every life. He stated that storms come to houses built on rocks as well as those on sand *(Mt 7:24-27).* If our expectations are that God should insulate us from the storms of life, we will be greatly disappointed. God has His own wise, just and loving timetable for our death.

Adversity Principle #33

God Knows What He Is Doing

"God understandeth the way thereof, and he knoweth the place thereof." Job 28:23

In chapter 28 Job relays his thoughts about the amazing world he lived in, *"Surely there is a vein for the silver, and a place for gold where they fine it. Iron is taken out of the earth, and brass is molten out of the stone" (Job 28:1, 2).* What incredible efforts mankind goes through to get riches. They plumb the depths of nature hoping to capitalize on iron, silver and gold. It is incredible what mankind can do when they want to. They can send people to the moon and back. They make all manner of technology that is simply mind baffling.

And yet, despite however much genius people acquire, they will never, ever understand why the wicked sometimes prosper and good people are punished. Matthew Henry said it this way, "…the caverns of earth may be discovered but not the councils of heaven."

With all our discoveries, why can't we humans figure out how to live wisely? The reason is because of our depraved human hearts. We simply don't want to seek God's ways. So God dishes out understanding slowly until we will appreciate His wisdom, *"Seeing it is hid from the eyes of all living, and kept close from the fowls of the air" (Job 28:21).* God and God alone knows what He is doing with this world, *"God understandeth the way thereof, and he knoweth the place thereof" (Job 28:23).* God knows why He does what He does.

Sometimes the things that hurt most help best

Many times in life I have started in one direction only to change direction and go the other way. Because of my humanity I don't always see clearly. But God always sees the perfect picture. He always acts according to His own purpose. God knows *what* He is doing and *why* He is doing it. We can have confidence that God sees where we can't and has a plan. Even in our deepest hurts, God can bring His healing.

Consider this blog from "Daily Thoughts" on the *Cornerstone Christian Church* Website:

"Chris Logan thought July 4, 2010 would be like any other Independence Day. With nothing on his calendar, he had every intention of sleeping in late before heading over to a friend's house for a holiday barbeque. His plans changed, however, when he got a call from Scott D'Annunzio. His friend had just scored a couple of passes to the nearby AT&T National golf tournament and wanted to know if Chris wanted to tag along. An avid PGA fan, Mr. Logan jumped at the chance to go out to the nearby Aronimink golf course to see some of his favorite players.

As luck would have it, Chris soon saw one of his favorites teeing up on the 18th hole. From his spot in *the gallery, Logan saw Sean O'Hair hit his final drive of the day. Unfortunately, he didn't see that the drive was headed straight for him. Before you could say "Fore!" Chris Logan was down on the ground after getting hit directly in the temple by O'Hair's errant shot.*

Medics quickly surrounded Chris, checking him for signs of a possible concussion. As they carried him off to a nearby medical tent for further observation, one of the doctors asked Chris about a small lump on his throat. Before discharging him, the doctor encouraged him to go and have that lump checked out. An appointment with an oncologist identified the lump as thyroid cancer. Six weeks and two surgeries later, Chris was well on his way to remission. The early diagnosis helped doctors eradicate the cancer before it spread anywhere else. Without the errant shot, there's no telling when doctors would have discovered the cancer or what they would have been able to do about it."

Sometimes, the things that hurt most help best. God is constantly working us over like a masterpiece of art. I've been to the doctor enough to know that wise pain can make us well. A scalpel may be as sharp as a dagger, but when wielded by a surgeon it becomes an instrument of healing.

I can remember sitting in Dr. Harju's History of Israel class during Bible College wondering to myself, why God's people (Israel) were so stupid! Over and over again they would do the same foolish thing. Finally, Dr. God had to apply the scalpel to the disease that was in them. God didn't want to hurt His people; He didn't want to cause them pain. But, it was in the midst of this same captivity that they would see their need for Him. God would use this terrible circumstance to heal and restore His people.

Though we live thousands of years after the fall of Judah, the same truth applies to us. God knows what He's doing. I know for me God used the painful circumstances of my life to point me back to Him in a way so much deeper than ever before. I recall a powerful moment for me on the last day of 2008. In addition to my wife's death, my mom passed away, a good friend committed suicide and our ministry was going through a serious attack of the devil. All of this in one year! As I was pouring out my heart to God I said to Him, "I am so done with this year...it's time to move on." In an instant, almost as though God had said audibly, "Are you done with Me too? Yes, you have had many troubles this year but have not those same tough times brought us closer than ever?!!!"

Instantly I felt deep conviction, "Yes" I thought to myself, "we *have* gotten closer than ever. I feel as though you and I have become friends, Lord. As much as I don't like the troubles, I LOVE Your presence! Forgive me God." We can trust our God. We can have confidence that God knows what He's doing. As Job reminds, "God understands the way."

Adversity Principle #34

Hold Your Blessings Loosely

"Moreover Job continued his parable, and said, Oh that I were as in months past, as in the days when God preserved me;" Job 29:1,2

It is remarkable how the winds of fortune can turn. One minute you feel like a king and the next a pauper! Job was mourning his former days of blessings. Job's lament is a good reminder to all of us not to hold on too tightly to the good times. Constantly bringing up and dwelling on the "months past" can only add to the pain of loss.

Holding our blessings loosely acts sort of like a "divine shock absorber"

Life changes. We should not imagine that life will

not transition. It does – and often quickly. In one twenty-four-hour period your life, as you know it, can become radically different. Job grudgingly shares some of the private details of his life. He doesn't like to do this but he does so for our benefit. "*Moreover Job continued his parable, and said, Oh that I were as in months past, as in the days when God preserved me" (Job 29:1, 2).* He said there was a time in his life when he felt the presence of God. He basked in the comfort of God. He sensed God's protection was around him. He saw the favor and blessing of God. It seemed like things were going his way, *"Then I said, I shall die in my nest, and I shall multiply my days as the sand" (Job 29:18).* Things were going his way. Even though he was not taking God for granted, he definitely wasn't ready for the size of the storm that flooded into his life. Who ever is?

Grief and loneliness are human emotions that are unpleasant but necessary. However, when many people encounter major losses in their lives they never get over them, because they are comparing yesterday's good times with today's challenges. Such comparison only causes us to get worse and sink deeper and deeper into despair.

Holding our blessings loosely acts sort of like a "divine shock absorber." Let me illustrate. Consider an automobile's shock absorbers. They're designed to cushion the vehicle from unexpected bumps in the road. Without them, the car would fall apart from the constant impacts encountered during its travels. Some vehicles, like a Cadillac, have extra cushioning. Others, like my 1958 Volkswagen, have none (or so it seems ☺)! People are like cars. We're traveling on the road of life, and most of the time, we're not expecting bumps or potholes. So when we suddenly run over one, we're not prepared for them. Giving our memories to the Lord in prayer cushions the blow, like a shock absorber, until we can readjust and adapt our thinking to accommodate the sudden change in the ride. Lament is normal. However, it becomes a major problem if people permanently refuse to let go.

Paul stated in *Philippians 3:13, "this one thing I do, forgetting those things which are behind, and reaching forth unto those things which are before."* Satan works to keep us from forgetting and out of the new place that God has for us. He wants to trap us with past memories and cause us to live in permanent misery.

If you are hurting right now due to memories of a loss in your life, you need to know that a new beginning is in front of you. You will go through some things that you'll never understand, but trust that as good as the past was, God has new days ahead. Hold every memory loosely and know that if God changes things up on you. He still has something good for you as you enter the future.

Adversity Principle #35

The Devil Will Attack When You Are At Your Lowest

"But now they that are younger than I have me in derision, whose fathers I would have disdained to have set with the dogs of my flock." Job 30:1

Job was hurt to the core of his existence. He was down. At such a time you would think he might get a break. But Satan added insult to injury. Job gets rather plain in his verbiage as he characterizes the people that are making his life miserable. Some misinformed and prejudiced people (and even their kids) were attacking Job's integrity. These people were so base, Job stated that he wouldn't even let them watch his dog!

There is a spiritual lesson to be learned in all of this – the devil will surely attack when you are down. So be alert! Satan is the most cunning creature that has ever existed. He has been studying human nature ever since Adam and Eve. He knows how people think and feel and discouragement is one of his oldest and best traps. He will spring it on you when you are at your weakest after the death of a loved one, or after a huge personal loss of some kind, when you feel all alone and unloved. The people Satan will send into your life at your weakest point will tempt you with your main weakness, and will confuse you with his/her seeming goodness.

When we are Hungry, Angry, Lonely or Tired is when we are most vulnerable to the attack of our archenemy, the devil - Charles Stanley

The devil will whisper to you through negative people who insinuate such things such as, "you might as well end it all now, because God doesn't love you." The devil attacks you when you are weak, and he is an opportunist. So if you're physically weak, tired, feeling great emotional or physical pain be prepared and be on guard!

Remember that the devil attacked Jesus when he was weak and hungry. He was attacked at His weakest point. The only response Jesus ever had to any of the devil's temptations was quoting the written Word of God. The devil did not give up however, Satan kept on hitting Jesus with thoughts of temptation repeatedly. The temptations were real and appealing. The devil seemed to offer an easier way than trusting and obeying God, but of course the devil is a liar.

The devil knows the right time to attack us. We are especially weak when our bodies feel very tired. Dr. Charles Stanley, noted pastor from Atlanta, mentions the H.A.L.T. principle he uses in his life. When we are Hungry, Angry, Lonely or Tired is when we are most vulnerable to the attack of our archenemy, the devil. It was certainly like this for Elijah too. Job found out that the devil knows no bounds of decency when it comes to our hearts.

You will just have to do your best to avoid the kind of people and situations that are instruments of Satan.

Spend time with godly people from your church instead. Stay alert in times of weakness. Understand your weaknesses and be prepared to recognize an attack and rebuke it with Scripture.

Adversity Principle #36

Some Things Are Unchangeable Through Human Effort

"Terrors are turned upon me: they pursue my soul as the wind: and my welfare passeth away as a cloud." Job 30:15

"I've been pursued by the hounds of heartache", Job cried. It's like trying to stop the wind from blowing. It's impossible. Tough times come to ALL humans despite every attempt to steer clear. To be sure there are some things about myself and my life that I *can* change. I can change many of my habits. I can change my hobbies. I can change my work ethic. Certainly, I can change my attitude (and changing that goes a long way)!

But you *cannot* change other things, such as your physical features. I also cannot change the sovereign providence of God. God's providence (His all-wise governing of all things for His glory and for your good) includes your losses, your ups, your downs, your good times and bad. God has a plan for good, despite how it feels, for you beyond this world that spans eternity. And that plan is unchangeable if you have trusted Christ as your Savior. If you belong to Christ, through trusting Him for salvation, then take Him by His nail scarred hand and let Him guide you.

Acceptance of God's wise plan requires faith and trust in a loving God whose purposes are often far beyond your expectations

Job knew he could not change the wind, *"Terrors are turned upon me: they pursue my soul as the wind: and my welfare passeth away as a cloud" (Job 30:15).* Time and time again clouds that gave a promise of cooler weather, just passed by. The reality of God's providence had taught him to accept God's perfect design for accomplishing His purposes for his life. As the prophet Isaiah said, *"O Lord, thou art our father; we are the clay, and thou our potter; and we all are the work of thy hand" (Isaiah 64:8).* God expresses Himself through His acts. The weaknesses, limitations, or difficulties caused by adversity can be used as tools in God's hands to achieve great things. As you accept (maybe not that you enjoy it) God's plan, you welcome His providence.

Acceptance of God's wise plan requires faith and trust in a loving God whose purposes are often far beyond your expectations. There are some things you cannot change. If you don't see an end in sight over the next week then go for a day. If you don't feel like you can make it for a day, then make it through the night, and if you don't feel like you can make it through the night then try to make it through an hour, and if you don't feel like you can make it through an hour then make it through five minutes. There are times when the suffering cuts so deep, when the heartache gets so painful, when things get so crazy that all you can do is just make it another few minutes. But if you can make it another few moments then KNOW this – somehow God will come through for you! That's all Job could hope for, because he knew there were just some things that only God can change.

Adversity Principle # 37

In The Midst Of Suffering You Must Make Extra Effort To Stand Guard Of Yourself

"I made a covenant with mine eyes; why then should I think upon a maid?" Job 31:1

When you are in the throes of adversity you must exert the extra effort in guarding yourself from sin. Job realized how much pain he was in and was looking for something to ease the pain. The thrill in the early stages of lust could be just too tempting, so he knew he needed some extra help in the form of a vow not to look at inappropriate things.

A man may find himself attracted to pornography to ease the pain of grief. A woman might be attracted to internet liaisons because of the emotional pain in her life. In the midst of heartache, immorality has a tendency to be an easy and attractive way to divert our minds from the pain. And so Job said he had to make a promise to himself, *"I made a covenant with mine eyes; why then should I think upon a maid..." (Job 31:1).* He started with his *eyes* but knew how important it was also to *think* on good things. Just when you *think* that the Word of God has a good hold on you and just when you *think* that you have sufficiently moved yourself away from immorality for years, the devil will bring unholy thoughts to your mind. Be watchful of this tendency in seasons of stress.

You also have to be careful about your attitudes and actions. It's all too easy to be unkind when you're suffering, *"If I did despise the cause of my manservant or of my maidservant, when they contended with me" (Job 31:13).* In periods of success we feel as though we don't need others and in periods of trouble we feel as though they're the ones causing our trouble. It's amazing how easily somebody else can become the "whipping boy" of every one of *your* problems.

Let me explain, let's say you're at work and you do something small, but your boss goes totally off…I mean just ballistic and you're thinking, "Wow, why is she so ticked off?" Well, you are just the current whipping boy. A week later it's going to be somebody else. The boss has deeper problems, but takes it out on you. And that's sometimes what we do with our own family. When we're not feeling good we kick our dog, are unkind to our children. We're abrupt with our wife and we're really mad at the telephone company. When we're not happy, *everybody* gets in our way. Job says I had to be careful about letting my mind go into immorality, but I also had to be careful about unkindness.

Finally, Job noted that the overzealous pursuit for wealth was a personal concern, *"If I have made gold my hope, or have said to the fine gold, Thou art my confidence…" (Job 31:24).* Job knew he had to be careful that he didn't go down the "riches at any cost" road and think that somehow money was going to buy him some relief from pain. Money never buys permanent relief from pain. All the lust…all the money in the world can't keep away suffering. That's something only God can do! And He delights to do so.

Adversity Principle #38

God Talks To Us Through Pain

"Then the Lord answered Job out of the whirlwind, and said" Job 38:1

Novelist and Christian apologist, C.S. Lewis said, "God whispers in our pleasures and shouts in our pain." Pain truly is a signal from God. Sometimes it is only in pain that we will stop and actually listen to God. It would be nice if life was always sunshine, but storms come. And when they do they carry a message, *"Then the LORD answered Job out of the whirlwind..." (Job 38:1).* Up to this point God hasn't spoken to Job's friends (or even to Job). But now God is going to speak loud and clear!

A Bible scholar once counted and found out that God asked Job 77 rhetorical questions in Job chapters 38-42. Now that's what I call getting into somebody's face! That would be like you or I sitting our son or daughter down and saying, "Where have you been? What's been going on? Who do you think's been paying your bills? Who do you think's been getting you up every morning? Who changed your diapers when you were a little baby?"

For hour after hour, question follows after question as God gives Job the "what for"! Now, for those who are new to scripture, this may seem like God is a bit callous. I mean, look at this picture – here is Job covered head to foot in scabs, his children are gone, his money has disappeared, his livelihood is destroyed and the first thing out of God's mouth is in essence, "Do you think that you know as much as Me?" *"Gird up now thy loins like a man; for I will demand of thee, and answer thou me. Where wast thou when I laid the foundations of the earth? Declare, if thou hast understanding…" (Job 38:3, 4).* God tells Job to man up because he had some "splainin" to do.

God thunders out about His sovereign plan for all mankind. God doesn't pull any punches, and the encounter is overpowering for Job. When I was a child, thunder and lightning would sometimes explode the skies, shake and rattle the whole house! It was an awesome display of God's incredible power. I can only imagine what it must have sounded like with God speaking from a whirlwind!

In the midst of his heartache, Job heard God clearly. Often times we are so busy with all of our fun, that we don't hear God. But when we are in pain, our ears are tuned in very clearly. When you are happy and so full of life that you have no sense of needing God, you have a tendency to be almost bothered by the voice of God. Grief saps the life right out of you. No matter what the source of your grief: death, illness, or loss of finances... the heartache you are suffering can be for your benefit as you begin to connect to God as never before.

Many people say they try to listen to God, but there is much confusion over discerning if you've truly heard God's voice. I know people who were sure they had heard God's voice and so they acted on it only to discover down the road that they were off base.

On occasion in Scripture God spoke audibly (like he did to Job), but in the vast majority of cases the way God speaks is by illuminating Biblical truth through thoughts or impressions that the Holy Spirit gives. The problem is, typically we can't hear the Holy Spirit over all the noise that is going on in our lives. It's kind of like being a parent and hearing the general "buzz" of our children's voices when all of a sudden we hear a cry of pain! The shriek of pain gets our attention…and fast. Hard times cut through the dull and din of everyday life to get our attention. I don't like pain, but I love being close to God!

I don't like pain, but I love being close to God!

God didn't speak out of the whirlwind to Zophar. God didn't speak to Bildad or anyone else but Job. He spoke only to Job. He spoke to Job because Job had a humble heart! He was willing to listen and was teachable. And even though Job had gotten out of line with his bad attitude at times, I get the sense in this whole thing - Job is like a person who has aged to the point where he finally realized he really didn't know diddly squat! You know what I mean…when you're 20, you know everything, and when you're 35 you know almost everything and as the years go by finally you wake up one day and say, "I don't know anything!"

God got through to Job in his pain and His main point was this – if you can't control a donkey, an eagle, or weather then maybe there are just some things you can't control in life. The answer? You have to trust God and just stay in constant communion with Him!

Adversity Principle #39

Never Argue With God

"Behold, I am vile; what shall I answer thee? I will lay mine hand upon my mouth." Job 40:4

The Christian bumper sticker I saw read, "God said it, I believe it, that settles it." That's a good plan. An even better plan is: "God said it, that settles it"! Job had to learn a good lesson – never ever argue with God.

The amazing thing about God is that He allows – to a point – for humans to express their pain; even their anger to Him

Never feud with God; you will lose every time! *"Then Job answered the LORD, and said, Behold, I am vile..." (Job 40: 3).* The Hebrew word "vile" translated by the King James translators here is not a suggestion of moral failure but rather of comparative insignificance. What Job had learned was that his understanding is nothing compared to God's.

Let's consider just one of the many examples of God's incredible wisdom from the animal kingdom. The "behemoth" is thought to be some kind of dinosaur, an animal that is one of the most dangerous, powerful and unconquerable of all the animals, *"Behold now behemoth, which I made with thee; he eateth grass as an ox" (Job 40:15).* Could you make a dinosaur a pet? No, but God can, because the hippo does everything He says.

Job responds to God's wise plan, "I know when I am beaten…dear God, you got me where you want me." *"I know that thou canst do everything, and that no thought can be withholden from thee. Who is he that hideth counsel without knowledge? Therefore have I uttered that I understood not; things too wonderful for me, which I knew not" (Job 42:2, 3)* Job states that he is sorry he argued with God, "I am ignorant…I spoke out of turn…I really don't understand your way…I believe you are my Savior...I thought I had things figured out and I had an idea of what's going on, but I didn't."

The amazing thing about God is that He allows – to a point – for humans to express their pain; even their anger to Him. In the Psalms we often see the author pouring out their "complaints" to the Lord, *"I poured out my complaint before him; I **shewed before him my trouble**" (Psa. 142:2).* In the end however you can't argue with God's plan. Too often we show our troubles only to ourselves, which only aggravates the problem. We mull over it and stew about it instead of giving it to God and then humbly submitting to His plan. The journey of grief for the Christian so often includes just submitting to God since we don't have all the facts to base an argument on.

The task of learning to accept the reality of loss, involves overcoming our denial. For me, this was initiated by viewing Lynette's body after her death, attending the funeral and then visiting the place where her body was laid to rest. It is necessary to grieve the physical finality of losing a loved one and come to grips with the fact that you will not see that person again in this life. As a Christian, I know that not only will I see her again in the life to come, but she is now in an immeasurably better place — in the Lord's presence, with no more pain, fear or sorrow. This is true for all who die in the Lord. Therefore, we are actually mourning for our loss, not for our Christian loved one.

What about my wife's death? Was it good? Well... yes and no. None of the evils of this world are "good", including the disease which took her life, but God *is* preparing us for a world where all wrong is made right. He is the Potter, we are the clay. He has the sovereign right to do with us whatever it takes to conform us into the image of Christ. When a loved one is taken away, and we cannot explain it we must not assume that God has no explanation and is limited in His ability to work good out of evil. Doubting God's plan is fruitless.

Every good gift comes from God. Lynette was a gift

to the family, the church and to myself. She was a gift we neither earned nor deserved. The appropriate response to a gift, even when it is taken away, is gratitude. Rather than dwell on the fact that she was taken away, I must be grateful that we shared life for 34 years. We can't argue with God.

Adversity Principle #40

Before Honor Is Humility

"So Eliphaz the Temanite and Bildad the Shuhite and Zophar the Naamathite went, and did according as the Lord commanded them: The LORD also accepted Job" Job 42:9

After Job gets a tongue lashing from God, he wisely repents. He repents genuinely and publicly *(42:6)*. There is no use trying to make excuses to God, since He knows everything already. The best policy is always honesty.

The Lord now turns to Job's friends, *"And it was so, that after the LORD had spoken these words unto Job, the LORD said to Eliphaz the Temanite, My wrath is kindled against thee, and against thy two friends: for ye have not spoken of me the thing that is right, as my servant Job hath" (Job 42:7).* I've got to imagine that those three friends were looking at Job at first and saying, "Yep, I told you...I told you God is mad at Job... HE'S REALLY upset with Job." I can see it now in my mind's eye. They were watching God tear into Job with all those seventy-seven questions and loving it! "Give it to him God! Yea, give it to him!" These friends were ecstatic and seemingly vindicated. It's like sitting in a church service and saying, "I hope brother Jones is hearing the preacher now. I hope sister Smith is listening because, boy I tell you what – they sure need it!" But unknown to them was the fact that God spoke to Job because he was the only one who would listen. Job had a humble heart. God had been trying to talk to these friends for the last 40 chapters...but these guys were too proud!

God then came face to face with his friends and commences to commence, "You guys are ticking me off, you're on my nerves now!" God speaks specifically to Eliphaz. Eliphaz was the first of the "speakers." Isn't it interesting how that when one person starts something negative, it just opens up a whole bunch of stuff.

Four different times in two verses *(42:7,8)* God calls Job His servant. I'm sure the friends thought, "Hey... wait, did I just hear you say Job was your servant; a man of God? Look at him. How can you call him a man of God?"

There is a good lesson to be learned here. Just because Job had lost it all didn't mean he was not God's servant. Just because he was down didn't mean he was out...just because he was at the lowest point of his life didn't mean that he was not loved by God. Through all of these conversations God was getting Job to a place where He could favor him. Before honor is humility. It's true – Job had had an attitude problem. At times he was surly, grouchy and hard to get along with. But you know what, I think we've got to give him some space. Job had been through a horrific life change.

God is not happy with those that mistreat and criticize His servants, *"Therefore take unto you now seven bullocks and seven rams, and go to my servant*

Job, and offer up for yourselves a burnt offering; and my servant Job shall pray for you: for him will I accept: lest I deal with you after your folly, in that ye have not spoken of me the thing which is right, like my servant Job" (Job 42:8). God points out that when you gossip about my servants you are griping about me! God tells Job's friends, "You've criticized my servant so you've criticized me. I don't even want to hear your excuses. You need an intercessor." That's what Job was good at, as we're told in the first chapter. He had been an intercessor for his family...he took God and man and brought them together.

Losing Lynette was painful...IS painful. But pain brings humility. Humility is not a passive quality. I have discovered that humility requires strength. It's an ability to stand before God's greatness and surrender to it, not out of weakness but out of respect, recognition, and awe of all that God is. Perhaps the strength of humility is the ability to bow to the wisdom of what we have experienced - to be humble enough to see the majesty of God's power in our lives, to be humble enough to see beyond our tears.

In one of the most beautiful passages in the Old Testament (Isaiah 61:2,3) it says that the Lord will, *"...comfort all that mourn. To appoint unto them that mourn in Zion, to give unto them beauty for ashes, the oil of joy for mourning..."* What a striking precious promise for those who are hurting due to loss.

Never forget that if the Lord has your life in ashes then the next step is BEAUTY!

In Biblical times, mourning was expressed in very tangible physical terms. The individual would tear the garments they wore, then they would throw ashes and dust on their head. They would remove their shoes and refrain from wearing nice clothes; dressing in sackcloth. Of course such physical expressions of humility are not necessary to meet with God. But bowing down before God, lying prostrate on the floor before God and weeping over sin in our lives or the lives of others still can have a powerful effect.

I once read that, "Life is one long lesson in humility."

I totally concur. God uses decade after decade of sanctified failures to continue to grow me. God is near to the humble. That is why God talked to Job but not his friends. Their pride put God off, as God *"...resisteth the proud" (James 4:6).* We gain healing through humility. Humility is dependence on Jesus Christ and the strong awareness that God is at work in all His love through my life.

Friend, where is your heart today? Are you wholeheartedly following Jesus Christ? Are you dependent on Him? Maybe circumstances or overwhelming temptations have all but shipwrecked your faith. Never forget that if the Lord has your life in ashes then the next step is BEAUTY! After humility comes honor.

Adversity Principle #41

Things Change When We Pray

"And the LORD turned the captivity of Job, when he prayed for his friends: also the LORD gave Job twice as much as he had before." Job 42:10

As long as Job was griping, and having a pity party God didn't turn His captivity. But when Job prayed, good things started happening! Notice *how* God accomplished this however, *"...the LORD turned the captivity of Job..."* God *turned* His captivity. Does this mean that God eliminated sickness? No. Does this mean that God gave him his money back? Not at this point. It just says that God *turned* his captivity. He had been held captive by the devil in the permissive will of God. Satan had Job in his net of adversity, trials and junk. Job couldn't break free from all the crud.

But when Job prayed for others, God started turning things around for him.

The single greatest thing we can do for another human is to pray for them! However, not only does the praying benefit others, but it is a benefit to ourselves as well.

Yes, God forgave the "pray-ees" but look what God did for the "pray-er" - Job. We go to prayer meetings and we get on our face before God praying for Him to do things for others, and God does do things for others, but the awesome thing is that God blesses the pray-er too!

In the New Testament the disciples saw Jesus and said, "Lord, teach us to pray." They never said, "Lord teach us to preach, or Lord teach us to administrate this great work that you have us doing." But they heard Him praying and said, "Oh my, teach us to pray like that." They saw the good that prayer was doing for those who were being prayed for. They could also see how communion with God was beneficial to Christ.

God turned things around for Job only after he prayed and when he did, God gave him twice as much as he had before! God will never be the debtor. He always pays back – with interest! *"Then came there unto him all his brethren, and all his sisters, and all they that had been of his acquaintance before, and did eat bread with him in his house: and they bemoaned him, and comforted him over all the evil that the LORD had brought upon him: every man also gave him a piece of money, and every one an earring of gold" (Job 42:11).* Many people that had previously pulled away from Job were now coming to his aid, bringing jewelry and money. Go figure! Once again we see how fickle people are – get used to it.

My broken heart made me passionate and I have found that passionate praying is the kind that gets the job done

President John Adams pointed out, "Grief drives men into habits of serious reflection, sharpens the understanding, and softens the heart." Most of us could pray more, I know I should. I have, for all of my adult life, had some time of prayer on a daily basis. But in an entirely new level, prayer became my passion. Grief drove me there in desperation. Prayer became a powerful antidote for my broken heart. As I would pray for my children, grandchildren and ministry, I could sense God was doing something inside me. Over time I have come to realize the powerful effect of prayer on my own heart. Prayer has a unique way of making you feel like you can win since God is hearing you, loosening the grip of grief.

Interestingly, every time I prayed a special request for someone else, I felt a little more strength in my own soul. Every time I felt weak, I just prayed a little more. I watched in awe as God worked answer after answer for others. My broken heart made me passionate and I have found that passionate praying is the kind that gets the job done, *"...The effectual fervent prayer of a righteous man availeth much" (James 5:16).*

For those left behind grieving for their loss, I know how painful it can be. I think back on one of the last conversations I had with my wife. Though she battled the symptoms of metastasized breast cancer for four years, it was about two weeks before she died that she specifically asked me to, "just pray that she could pass quickly." She was looking forward to seeing her Lord! I remember the peace of God behind her words when she asked for that prayer. I understood in that moment that she didn't need fancy or poetic words, what she longed for was fervent prayer.

There are many helpful things that can be done for someone that is grieving, but the greatest is prayer. The one component that Christians can provide that secular people cannot is the power of prayer!

When Christians pray not only do things begin to happen for good…they themselves are strengthened. Friend, don't worry about it, pray about it. As the late Pastor Chuck Smith said, "Turn worry time into prayer time."

I discovered that there is a sacredness in grief that I found in no other circumstance. As long as you live there will be a sacred place in your soul to go to for prayer. A continual "limp" as Anne Lamont put it:

"You will lose someone you can't live without, and your heart will be badly broken, and the bad news is that you never completely get over the loss of your beloved. But this is also the good news. They live forever in your broken heart that doesn't seal back up. And you come through. It's like having a broken leg that never heals perfectly – that still hurts when the weather gets cold, but you learn to dance with the limp."

Adversity Principle #42

Never Give Up, Because Something Good Is Coming

"So the LORD blessed the latter end of Job more than his beginning..." Job 42:12

For those that have faith in God and for those that believe God, something good is always ahead. God is sometimes pleased to make the end of a person's life more comfortable than the former has been, *"So the LORD blessed the latter end of Job more than his beginning..." (Job 42:12).*

The literal facts of Job's restoration are phenomenal, if not humorous. From all the specifics given in the last chapter of Job's story, we can see that God doubled everything that he had previously, *"...for he had fourteen thousand sheep, and six thousand camels, and a thousand yoke of oxen, and a thousand she asses" (Job 42:12).* Double the amount that was detailed in chapter One. That is just remarkable! But now notice an even more amazing fact – God gives him ten more children, *"He had also seven sons and three daughters" (Job 42:13).* How old was Job at this time? Well, if all his blessings were in doubles and he lived to be 140 – then he was seventy at the time of his turnaround. That means then from age seventy to age 140 he had ten more children…now that's what I call a blessing! There is sort of a poetic justice in all of this as well. It's obvious that Job and his fussing wife were restored, as they had more children. If she was the same age as Job, she had ten more pregnancies *after* the age of seventy (God is sovereign☺).

Another interesting fact is that God doesn't list the names of any of the boys, he only lists the name of three daughters, *"And he called the name of the first, Jemima; and the name of the second, Kezia; and the name of the third, Kerenhappuch" (Job 42:14).* I think one obvious reason God did this was because

He would teach a lesson through the meaning of the names of Job's daughters. "Jemima" means "the day." God, out of Job's darkness, gave him a new day. "Kezia" which means "spice", reminded Job of a pleasant and fragrant smell because God had healed him and his prayers were a sweet smell to God. "Kerenhappuch" means, "the plenty is restored." God had restored Job greater than ever! Amen and amen.

In all the land there were no women "so fair." Does that mean they were pretty? I'm sure they were of beautiful countenance but actually it means that there were no women so *virtuous* as the daughters of Job. It was obvious that God blessed these precious girls because of their father. His integrity touched their lives. Certainly the sons were blessed too, but there was something about these girls whose lives were made virtuous by the life of their father.

Job went on to live a full and greatly used life even after the loss of those people and things that were so special in his life, *"...and saw his sons, and his sons' sons, even four generations. So Job died, being old and full of days" (Job 42:16-17).* Being older is one thing but being "full of days" is another. I want every day to be *full* of God and *full* of usefulness and *full* of the blessing, favor and joy of the things of God. What good is it to live if we're not going to be full of the grace of God. He lived to be at least a 140 years old and saw God bless four or five generations.

I have never experienced heavier grieving then when it became apparent that God was taking Lynette, my childhood sweetheart for 7 years and wife of 34 years, home to Himself. I have had friends disappoint me, I have had lifestyle dreams evaporate. However, when the most sacred of earthly relationships ended, it shattered my world. There were pieces of my life and heart everywhere. It was, to put it mildly, terrible.

How did I get through this time? I knew from Scripture that God still had good things ahead for me, despite what my head was saying and my broken heart was feeling.

I remember watching Charlie Brown years ago on

TV. He always walked around with a negative slant on life. I didn't want to do that, but it was hard not to. Everybody has grieved, is grieving or will someday grieve a loss so big that it seems as though you will never see another day of sunshine. Yet I have learned that we all have a choice about how we will react to the loss. Instead of letting the devil steal your tomorrow, I encourage you to grab hold of the future.

Your relationship with God makes it possible. He gives the grace to do anything with His help. Better days are ahead. Romans 8:37-39 says, *"Nay, in all these things we are more than conquerors through him that loved us. For I am persuaded, that neither death, nor life, nor angels, nor principalities, nor powers, nor things present, nor things to come, Nor height, nor depth, nor any other creature, shall be able to separate us from the love of God, which is in Christ Jesus our Lord."* Now isn't that a better outlook than the Charlie Brown mentality. God *is* on your side! He will guide us and protect us because His love is perfect. God has a new future. It might not be one that you planned for, but it is good. Good things are just ahead...they really are. Just you wait and see!

Trusting God

by Pauline Pollock

My husband Mike and I were married at an early age. God blessed us with three children, and for nearly four decades, we were constantly growing and learning to trust God in every challenging life situation we faced. The biggest test of my faith was when Mike became seriously ill. He had struggled with diabetes for years, and then fought hepatitis C and the side effects from its treatment. Often at the close of the church service, my son Andrew and I would go to the altar to pray for his healing, not realizing at the time what kind of healing God would ultimately bring. When Mike told me he felt he would die young, I would complain, "No, you can't leave me! You have a young son."

The string of events that preceded his death is unforgettably etched in my mind. It was Thanksgiving, and on the way to my oldest daughter and son-in-law's home, I noticed he was abnormally cold. Throughout the day, he never complained or mentioned how bad he was feeling. That night his condition worsened, and we had to call an ambulance to take him to the hospital. He was stabilized and after a few days discharged on Wednesday. But by Friday evening, his condition worsened, and we had to take him back to the hospital. It was that night, December 6th, that he passed on into eternity.

I was in shock and disbelief at the speed of events and the unexpected finality of his death. Worse yet, the holidays were now upon us, but we were certainly not in a holiday mood. It was so hard just to function! I still wanted to make Christmas special for the grandkids, so I went to the dollar store, bought big bags and just let my young son Andrew fill them up with whatever stuff he though they would like. But my most trying time didn't occur until after the funeral, when my mom, who was visiting from Colorado, went back home. That is when the loneliness overwhelmed me. I had no idea who I was. I had been married right after high school and lived with Mike for thirty-five years. My life had been in terms of "us" and now all of a sudden, life was all on me: to pay the bills, to make housing choices, to raise my son (My daughters were married by then).

Many confusing emotions and baffling actions took place in the months that followed. Things like going off and leaving our house door wide open while in Yosemite, or mailing checks alone in an envelope without the paperwork. I would even drive around in circles not knowing how to get where I was going. I would see fathers with their sons, and just cry. I would hear a heart moving song in church and have to leave the service, overcome with grief. Sometimes I would be going down the aisles of a store, and hear one of Mike's favorite songs over the music system and waves of fresh grief would return.

Yet through it all, even as those waves of grief washed over me, I could still see and feel the hand of God on me. I felt Jesus so close to me. During this time I was learning two huge lessons.

First lesson: ***Trust God***

"Be still and know I am God" (Psa. 46:10) was a verse God gave me that reinforced Him as my anchor. He continually comforted me. That's not to say that made it easy and I didn't have any challenges. Besides learning to navigate life as a single person, I was especially concerned over the rearing of my son, who was ten at the time of Mike's death. Yet, I realized it was God who allowed this in my life, so I trusted Him – I had to. He gives and takes away. I prayed for mentors, and God brought some godly men alongside to befriend him, help with school-work and do "guy type" activities like going to a baseball game. Where I felt so inadequate, God made a way to compensate for it.

The story doesn't end there though, for God certainly has a way of writing last chapters. I thought I would live out my life single, and was content with that, if that's what God wanted. I never could have imagined what would happen next, not in a million, billion years! A few years after Mike died, my Pastor of twenty-five years, lost his wife, Lynette. After that it seemed as though God put a spot light on me. Tim and I were already friends and co-laborers, but now our friendship became a "special friendship." It was during a small group at our church that I learned my next great lesson.

Second lesson: ***God has great plans for us***

In this group we were studying the "Prayer of Jabez" (1 Chron. 4:10). After the class was over, I prayed for God to enlarge my borders. I already had some of my grandchildren to care for much of the time, so I thought that what He was planning for me, but God had even bigger plans of which I had no idea.

One day Pastor (Tim) asked me an important question that would change everything. He came up to me and asked, "Do you text?" Well, that led up to, "Do you mind if we go over a book together? Can I call you to discuss it?" Tim gradually moved from being my Pastor to being my "special friend." He started the courting process and was romantic, attentive, fun and confident. We spent time on the phone getting to know each other. At first, I must admit, I thought to myself that this was weird, even bizarre. Then gradually the awkwardness faded and it became easier and felt more natural to be around each other. Although at times it still seemed surreal, I could see and feel that God was pushing me towards Tim. I had to let go of the future I had envisioned. This was God "enlarging my borders" and writing an unexpected new chapter in my life book.

When the day came we finally married, it was both exciting and scary! We felt we were stepping out in the direction God was leading us, but knew we would face challenges that come with combining two households. Now looking back I can say wholeheartedly what a sweet blessing life has been with his four sweet teen girls and my young teen son (at the time). It has been such a different lifestyle, but God has been so faithful as He has helped me grow and change for His glory and ministry. While I have had to rethink things and surrender areas, God is always "my God, my strength, in whom I will trust; my buckler (shield)" - Psalm 18:2. My life is a living testimony to the grace of God through my journey of grief; a journey that has taken me to a place in life far more blessed and loved than I could have ever imagined.

A Short, Bible Message from Mike Robinette...

If you were to die today, do you know for sure where you would spend eternity?

My friend, you have just been presented the most important question you will ever be asked. I know, because someone who cared for my soul asked me this question when I was in my early twenties. Finding the answer to this question was the single most life changing experience in my life! May I please share my testimony with you?

This friend showed me it is possible to be religious, go to church, be baptized, try to do good, and still not have eternal life! I saw from God's Word that there are four steps one must believe and accept in their heart in order to go to Heaven.

FIRST STEP is admitting that you are a sinner! Romans 3:23 says, "*For all have sinned and come short of the Glory of God.*" We do not deserve Heaven! God demands us to be sorry for our sins and to repent. Luke 13:3

SECOND STEP is realizing you owe a penalty for your sin. Romans 6:23 says,"*For the wages of sin is death, but the gift of God is eternal life through Jesus Christ our Lord.*" Anyone who rejects God's forgiveness through his Son will be separated from God forever in Hell as made clear in Revelation 20:14.

THIRD STEP is that you must believe that Jesus Christ paid the penalty for you with His own blood. Romans 5:8-9 says, *"But God commendeth (displayed) his love toward us, in that, while we were yet sinners, Christ died for us...being now justified by his blood, we shall be saved from wrath through him."* Only Jesus can forgive us and give eternal life.

FOURTH STEP is you must believe that Jesus Christ is God in the flesh, who came and died for our sins and rose again the third day. Romans 10:9 says, *"That if thou shalt confess with thy mouth the Lord Jesus, and shalt believe in thine heart that God hath raised him from the dead, thou shalt be saved."* Ask Jesus to come into your heart and be your Savior. Romans 10:13 says *"For whosoever shall call upon the name of the Lord shall be saved."* My friend, right now you are faced with the most important decision in your life. Will you say yes or no to Jesus? The Lord wants to save you. **Will you pray this prayer as I did when I received Christ?**

"Dear Jesus, I know I am a sinner who deserves hell. I believe you paid for my sins with your own blood to save me. Dear Lord, please forgive me of all my sins and come into my heart right now and save me. In Jesus' name, Amen."

- Rev. Mike Robinette

ABOUT MIKE...

Mike Robinette gave his life to the Lord at the age of twenty-four in Southern California after living the "hippie" lifestyle and serving in the U.S. Army during the Vietnam War. By God's grace, Mike realized that Jesus Christ is the Savior of the world and the answer to life.

Mike & Linda Robinette
evangelmiker@peoplepc.com

Today, Mike is sent out by The Home Church as a missionary evangelist to India & America.